CONTENTS

ACKNOWLEDGEMENTS

Many people have helped, directly and indirectly, in the research and preparation of this book. In particular, there are many friends in Jakarta, Yogyakarta and elsewhere – we were all students together, once upon a time – they are too many for me to name, but I am grateful to all of them. I should particularly like to mention the following, as long as it is understood that they are not responsible for whatever errors have made their way into my text. First, my five sisters: Sumarni Syamsi in Magelang, Central Java; Harmini Djamil in Bandung; Ratnasari and her husband Haikal Salam, in Pontianak, West Kalimantan; Roslina Usman in Jakarta; and Nurmalina Anwar, also in Pontianak. My brother-in-law, Usman Beka, gave me a lot of help in introducing me to people and making my travel arrangements, while Nurdiana Basuki patiently found books for me and answered innumerable questions. Among many friends in Yogyakarta, I must record the names of Soeatminah and of Ahmad Wirono and his wife. In Bali, Anak Agung Gde Rai and his wife, and Suryasih Mudita were especially helpful and hospitable.

In Bangkok, I received help, generosity and encouragement from two old friends, formerly of the Thai Section at the BBC, Kamolvan Punyashthiti and Sombat Bhuapirom, and from Mrs Punyashthiti's mother, Kunying Thavil Prakop Nitisar. They took enormous trouble to make sure that I saw and tasted everything, and they introduced me to dishes, recipes, restaurants and chefs that were vital to my purpose in writing the book.

In London, I should like to thank my two editors, Gill Cormode and Veronica Sperling, who have put a lot of their own enthusiasm into the book as well as their professional expertise. Another old friend who has contributed a great deal to my knowledge of Indonesian cooking is Fatimah Yahya. Several of these recipes came originally from her.

As ever, I owe much to Alan Davidson, who published my previous book, *Indonesian Food and Cookery*, and who has kindly contributed a Foreword to this new book. I may mention, by the way, that the great bulk of information in this book, and all but one or two of the recipes, are quite new and did not appear in *Indonesian Food and Cookery*. Thao Soun has made some new drawings with the exquisite accuracy of detail and lightness of touch that I, among many others, so much admire.

Sri Owen
Wimbledon
14 April 1988

Bamboo flute

FOREWORD

A new book by Sri Owen is a happy event, and I embrace the opportunity to celebrate it.

It is not just that she is a marvellously good cook and a fine writer; nor just that her amiable personality suffuses what she writes with a special charm. There is a further cause for celebration. The cuisines of which she writes, unlike those of most European countries and North America, have not been the subject of lots and lots of books. Much remains to be told.

Living and travelling in South-East Asia in the mid-1970s, I quickly realised how good the food was, and how varied from country to country and region to region. I also discovered the paucity of good written material about it. In many European countries there is a long line of cookery books stretching back to the Middle Ages. Not so in South-East Asia.

This contrast does not reflect a lack of material. A dispassionate comparison of the cuisine of, say Spain with that of Thailand, or the Netherlands with Indonesia, or England with Malaysia, is quite enough to show that. Yet, because of the lack of books, the cuisines of South-East Asia have until recently attracted less attention than they deserve.

Returning to England from Laos with a certain evangelical zeal for things South-East Asian, and accidentally becoming a publisher, I was really pleased that the first book to emerge from our infant publishing house, in 1980, was Sri Owen's *Indonesian Food and Cookery*, an expanded version of the book by her which Faber had had the foresight to publish some years earlier. This has been expanded yet again (1986) and is, I believe, both the best and the most user-friendly book on the subject. The enjoyable experience of producing and marketing it brought home to me how many users there are and how much they appreciate its merits.

Anyone dealing with a part of South-East Asia is bound to be tempted to cross national boundaries and explore neighbouring parts. The countries are like a string of jewels, or rather strings, for one can link them in various ways. One string starts in the Asian sub-continent and goes from Burma to Thailand and on to Malaysia and Indonesia and the Philippines. As in the game of 'Chinese whispers', the starting point and the end are dissimilar; but at each step there are clear similarities to be observed. The web of influences and connections would take a lifetime to disentangle, especially if the pervasive influence of China and the Chinese overseas communities were taken into account, plus culinary currents flowing from the Indian sub-continent and weird relics from colonial regimes; and most people would rather just enjoy the dishes than probe into their history. All the same, it is very interesting to have two of the cuisines juxtaposed, as in this book, and to sense something of their relationship.

My interest is all the greater because the book is right up to date. Too often, a cuisine is treated as something which has taken its definite and final shape, rather than as something which is organically growing and changing with every passing year. Sri Owen is one of those authors who recognise that history is today as well as yesterday and who are alert to current trends. Reading her introduction, I realise that my own memories of eating in Thailand and Indonesia, more than ten years old, are already out of date in some respects. Everything happens faster in South-East Asia!

Thai restaurants have now sprung up in many western countries, some more authentic than others but all offering an introduction to a truly rich cuisine. The size of their menus is a good indicator of this. The one nearest to my home has always, in the fifteen years we have been going to it, offered over a hundred dishes – and none of them comes from a caterer's frozen pack via a microwave oven. Nor are we expected to treat them with awe. Thai food is for enjoyment, and the people who serve it create the right mood with their charming smiles and elegant Thai dress.

For me the most wonderful Thai restaurant is, and I think will always be, the Rung Taw Kitchen in a quiet *soy* (side street) in bustling Bangkok. It is like eating in a private home; indeed it is, for that is where M. L. Taw Kritakara lives. Her welcome, and the beauty of the rooms and the table settings and the food, create a feeling of deep, tranquil happiness. Reading recently Theodore Zeldin's masterwork on Happiness, and prompted thereby to think of fragments of pure happiness in my own life, I found my mind going back to this restaurant, where I was drinking *khing sot* (the fresh ginger drink) and passing on from an exquisite fish dish to the special dessert: *manglak* (sweet basil) seeds in coconut milk.

The dish in which the fish was presented was itself exquisite, as well as the fish, and I told M. L. Taw so. Before we left, she gave me beautifully wrapped packages containing two of these dishes, gifts for me and my wife, permanent reminders in our own dining room to keep items of Thai fare on our menu and Thai ingredients in stock – coriander, ginger, galingale, *nam prik* (the chilli sauce which antedates the arrival of the chilli pepper in Thailand in the 16th century, for it was previously made with indigenous peppers), lemon grass, garlic, shrimp paste, etc., etc.

The time I spent in Indonesia was largely devoted to the pursuit of seafood dishes, of which I am glad to see that Sri Owen gives a generous selection in this book. I'm not sure whether anyone has ever calculated the total coastline which Indonesia's thousands of islands provide, but it must be the largest by far in South-East Asia. To chronicle in full the wealth of Indonesian seafood dishes would constitute a very agreeable life's work for someone. I was well aware that I was only catching a tiny percentage in my own trawl, but what a pleasure this was! I remember

particularly having a fish dinner one balmy evening at Pelabuhan Ratu, sitting in a cliff-top garden and looking out over the Indian Ocean with nothing but sea between us and Antarctica, and no sound but that of waves ending their long journey by breaking on the beach below.

However, there are many other important aspects to Indonesian food and cookery, not least the amazing range of fermented products of the soya bean which Indonesians have elaborated. Tempeh, which is their own invention, is one which is becoming increasingly popular in western countries; not surprising, since it is one of those foods which combine truly remarkable nutritional qualities with excellent taste and texture.

Foodstuffs and ways of cooking must occupy a focal place in any cuisine, but there are other important elements, such as markets, restaurants, street foods, eating habits, forms of hospitality and so forth. In all these respects the cuisines of South-East Asia are a delight, and none more delightful than that of Indonesia. Wayside food stalls are found in many countries, but the *warung* in Indonesia has a special charm, as my own observations and description given by Sri Owen elsewhere demonstrate:

> 'Architecturally, it is extremely simple: a roof, a table-cum-counter and a bench are the essentials. The counter is almost hidden under tiers of glass bottles and glass-fronted tins containing cakes, *krupuk, emping*, biscuits, nuts, sweets, *rempeyek*, dried fruit – dried fish, dried meat, or *dendeng* – anything, in short, that will keep. There are bottles of brightly coloured *stroop*, or syrupy sweet drinks. Somewhere behind or below this display the cooking goes on, and customers stand, sit on the bench, or squat on the ground nearby.'

I was also delighted by the practice which I found in the ubiquitous Padang restaurants (the name is taken from a town in Sumatra), where dishes of everything available are placed on the table as soon as one sits down. Instead of waiting while one's family or guests pore over a menu and ask questions about it, one can just say 'help yourselves'. This is a real time-saver, and I hope that the tradition will be maintained. I was slightly alarmed to read in this new book that in private homes, at least urban ones, the similar practice of laying just about everything out at once is giving way to the serving of courses in sequence. However, that is what Sri Owen does in her own home, where I have enjoyed many a delicious meal, and I can see its advantages.

In an essay written not so long ago, M. F. K. Fisher sounded a warning, disconcerting, note about people 'who love to cook'. Under her remorseless analysis, the statement 'I love to cook' is perceived to have hidden meanings such as 'I love power, and control of the kitchen gives it to me'. No doubt M. F. K. Fisher is right, in a general way, but I wish that she could meet Sri Owen, for I am sure that she would at once admit that here is an exception, a cook who in a completely uncomplicated way really does just love to cook – and to share her knowledge and enthusiasm with all of us.

Alan Davidson
Chelsea
July 1988

INTRODUCTION

This book is full of recipes, but it is really about food. I have no special wish to start people making monster *rijsttafels* or hunting exotic spices for authentic ethnic meals. The recipes are authentic, of course, but ingredients should be quite easy to find in most large towns in Britain and North America and Australia. By all means cook complete Indonesian or Thai meals – you can scarcely go wrong! But my real purpose is to introduce ingredients, flavours, techniques. Anyone who cooks their way through this book will, I think, develop a real insight into the way we cook and eat in Indonesia and Thailand today – not so much in the villages, where tradition is still strong, but in the big cities where all sorts of interesting changes are happening: folkways developing into lifestyles, new cuisines growing out of the old.

For example, it used to be the custom to put all the food on the table at once and let everyone help themselves. The 'help yourself' rule still applies, but the average family meal is now often served in a sequence of courses, and the total number of dishes is nowadays smaller than it used to be because when the housewife (or her husband) cooks there is not enough time to make anything too elaborate. Another development: the availability of imported foodstuffs, and the increasing popularity of cookery columns in magazines, has helped to make foreign food fashionable, and Italian dishes (for instance) may turn up on the table alongside local ones.

This seems to me an excellent approach to catering for the family and for parties, and any of the dishes in this book will fit very happily into a menu, which may

Market stall in Yogyakarta

otherwise be pure European, or Chinese, or Mexican or what you will. As with my previous books, I have cooked all the dishes in this book and if you follow the recipes exactly you will get excellent results – but once you are familiar with the things we do to food, then adapt and improvise, invent your own variations on Thai curries and Indonesian *sambal goreng*. It's time we stopped thinking of 'our' food and 'foreign' food – as has been so often said of music, what matters is knowing what's good.

Thai and Indonesian food have much in common, and it seems sensible to put them together in one book. There would be no excuse, though, for blurring the differences. Some ingredients are available in one country and not in the other; for example, there are no *kemiri*, or candlenuts, in Thailand. There are differences in taste: Indonesians dislike coriander roots and leaves, and use only the seeds. Religion and custom play important roles in eating habits. Most Thais are Buddhists, and are very willing to eat pork – those who are not vegetarians. Most Indonesians are Moslems and avoid pork. They consider lamb or goat their favourite meat, while the Thais seem not to eat lamb at all, except in the region close to the Malaysian border. But both nations have very similar climates, soils, fruits and vegetables, and both societies are changing fast.

I did all the research for this book in big cities – Bandung, Jakarta, Bangkok – and large provincial capitals: Yogyakarta in Central Java, Pontianak in West Kalimantan. I have read somewhere that these cities are among the fastest-growing in the world, and I can believe it. The pace and the pressures are ruthless, exciting, frightening. Yogyakarta still has something of the atmosphere of cultured politeness that I remember from my student days there. Pontianak was a fishing village for centuries and later the seat of a minor Sultan. Now, with its broad river bringing logs and barges from the interior, and the fine new bridge taking the coast road across that river, it seems set to become the sago and plywood capital of the world.

In two words: traditions change. Wherever I went, I enjoyed lavish hospitality, as has always been our custom. I met friends and friends' friends and was asked into their houses and their kitchens, and I met restaurant owners, hotel managers, journalists, editors and publishers. From what they told me and showed me, I began to get some notion of the changes that are taking place, and of the underlying attitudes that are unchanged.

People's expectations are much higher than they were. Thirty years ago, if your house had electricity at all, you thought yourself lucky to have 40 watts – enough for one small light bulb. Today my sisters and their friends take it for granted that they will be able to run a fridge and perhaps a food processor as well as ample lighting and the inevitable colour TV and video recorder. Electric ovens are becoming fairly common, though freezers are still rare, perhaps because of running costs.

In the shops, you can buy imported foods – things like cheese and apples – which are by no means cheap today but which, in the sixties, were scarcely to be found anywhere. And the local produce is as fine as ever, especially (it seemed to me) the fruits that won't travel – above all the durian. Durian, even in season, has become horribly expensive, but who cares? With my sister and her husband, we drove out to Bogor and filled the back of the jeep with durian lashed together in fours, and with freshly-cut Bogor pineapples that smell as sweet and innocent as the durian smells corrupt.

It is the 'middle classes', of course – still a small minority in the population but far more numerous and better-off than I remember them – who are making a social revolution. Their attitudes to food, on the other hand, have not changed as much as may appear. There are Kentucky Fried Chicken franchises in all the big towns, because any fried chicken has been a favourite dish since time began; but McDonald's had not, at least when I was in Jakarta in late 1987, got a foothold in Indonesia because (I was told) people suspected that minced-up burger meat might conceal pork.

And the domestic traditions remain. Food is bought fresh whenever possible, though the daily visit to the market, which I used to enjoy so much in the cool of early morning, has been replaced by a weekly or twice-weekly trip to load up the car. Food is never wasted if it can possibly be saved and used. Domestic pets eat up the leftovers. My pampered London cat insists on meat; Indonesian cats seem to thrive on rice. Guests are welcomed at any time, invited or not; those who are invited may bring others with them, or may not turn up at all. Servants and hangers-on are fed; one great lady I met in Bangkok provides lunch every working day for the staff of her son's garage business – 180 of them.

In the long run, the big change is that the housewife tends to leave much less to the cook than she used to, while her husband and children may well come into the kitchen to help or to take over. Cookery books, virtually unknown before the war, are now best sellers and cookery journalism is becoming big business.

This active interest in cooking needs to be seen as only a small part of the day's work. Wives, in Thailand and Indonesia, have careers; this is partly because they need the money but mostly because they have never submitted to being housebound by chores and children. Even one servant gives a wife a lot of freedom. But with only one, the family must do something for themselves, and cooking is most people's first choice. There's also the health angle, of course. The more diet-conscious people become, the stronger their desire to get into the kitchen.

So, inevitably, there arises a demand for convenience food, recipes that are quick and easy to make, ingredients that have been processed before they are bought. You can see the changes in the markets – not just the new supermarkets in the city centres, which are becoming pretty much like the ones I am used to in London, but the much older street markets and those in smaller towns as well. Side by side with whole coconuts, coriander seeds and chillies are grated coconut flesh, ground coriander and crushed chillies, prepacked in little plastic bags. How hygienic the new ways are is debatable, but they are a boon to those without food processors. In Denpasar, the capital of Bali, you can buy spices in exactly the quantities you need for the dish you are going to cook, and ask the meat-seller in the market to cut the meat appropriately and even to advise you on ingredients and method.

I suspect, though, that this is a survival of tradition rather than an innovation. It sounds like the sort of thing you find in a society without cookbooks, where memory is helped out by improvisation. Since my first book was published, I have had some very interesting and helpful letters from readers, some of whom queried ingredients, methods or the names of dishes. I am sure they are right (for the part of Indonesia they are familiar with), just as I think I am right for the areas that I know well. In this book, however, I make no pretence of doing things just as they were done, or are done, in any particular place. I have included notes on spices and sauces that may be unfamiliar to western readers, but if some ingredients are not available to you, don't hesitate to substitute according to your imagination and experience. The result may not be strictly 'authentic', but it will be well-cooked, interesting and delicious.

SPECIALITY INGREDIENTS AND SUBSTITUTES

Beancurd

Indonesian, *tahu*; better known perhaps in the west by its Japanese name, *tofu*. This soft, cream-coloured paste or gel is prepared from soya beans and is full of nutrients. It can be obtained in most good oriental food stores and healthfood shops, either fresh, fried, packeted or in kit form. Fresh beancurd sold in 500 g blocks has a short life; kept cool, and submerged in water, it will last for three or four days. Fried beancurd, sold in packets of 6 or 8 blocks each of 1 oz (30 g) must also stay cool, but not in water; it will last about a week. 'Everlasting' or 'silken' beancurd will keep for a year or more, even without refrigeration, provided the packet is not opened; once open, it must be used within a day or two. It will do for cooking, but is a bit runny. Kits are marketed by some Japanese makers, and you can make quite good fresh beancurd with them. However, I would always choose the real stuff, freshly made, whenever possible.

Candlenuts (*Aleurites moluccana*)

Indonesian, *kemiri*. These are very similar to macadamia nuts, but not quite the same. They are used in many Indonesian recipes, always crushed or ground before being mixed with other ingredients. Raw macadamia are a satisfactory substitute. Most Far Eastern food shops now stock them. Don't eat candlenuts raw – they are mildly toxic until cooked.

Chillies (*Capsicum annuum, C. frutescens*)

Indonesian, *cabé*; Thai, *prik*. Although chillies are so important in South-East Asian cooking today, they were only introduced to this area in the sixteenth century, when seeds and plants were brought from Central America. There are of course several kinds of chilli. The two things to remember are: the smallest chillies are the hottest; and the hottest part of the chilli is the seeds. That's why many of these recipes tell you to take the seeds out. Chillies can irritate the skin, especially if you are not accustomed to handling them. Rub a little salt on your hands before you start cutting them up, and wash your hands afterwards. Keep your hands away from your face and eyes while working with chillies. If you do get a little of the juice in your eye, it will smart uncomfortably; wash the area with plenty of cold water. See also page 118.

Coconut, coconut milk

Indonesian, *kelapa*; Thai, *maprao*. Coconuts play a central role in the cooking of South-East Asia. Genuinely young ones, alas, are rarely available in Europe. (I once had one in my shop – it was a lovely fresh green, but it must have been lying about its age because one morning it exploded and spattered everything and everybody with fermented coconut water.) The 'fresh' brown hairy ones you buy in the supermarket are fine, and for a few of these recipes I think it is worth the trouble of cracking one open and prising out the flesh. This always comes away from the shell with a brown skin on its surface. If the flesh is to be used for making coconut milk, this brown skin need not be cut away because its colour will not affect the finished dish. If, however, the flesh is to be used in a salad or a sweet, the brown skin should be removed and discarded before grating the coconut.

Coconut milk For most dishes, the 'coconut milk' that is specified (*santen* in Indonesian, *nam katee* in Thai) is not the liquid that you can drink from a newly-opened nut, but is the milk extracted from the flesh. It can easily be made from fresh grated coconut (that is how we make it in countries where coconuts and labour are plentiful), but in the west it is more conveniently made from desiccated coconut. *If you use fresh grated coconut,* one nut will make about 1 pint (600 ml) of medium-thick milk. Pour hot water over the grated flesh and leave to stand until luke-warm. Then press and squeeze the flesh to extract the milk, and pass through a sieve to separate the liquid. The more water you use, the thinner the milk will be; the recipe should specify thick (or thin) coconut milk.

Coconut milk from desiccated coconut To make thick coconut milk, use 12 oz (350 g) of desic-cated coconut and 1 pint (600 ml) of water, as described below. Then follow the same procedure again, using the same amount of water, to make a thin coconut milk. By mixing the two extractions you will get a medium thick coconut milk which is the standard thickness for most dishes.

(1) With a blender Put the desiccated coconut into the blender and pour on *half* the water, which should be hand-hot. Run the blender for 20–30 seconds, then pass the mush through a fine sieve, squeezing and pressing the coconut flakes as dry as you can. Put the coconut back into the blender, add more water and repeat the blending and sieving.

(2) Without a blender Put the desiccated coconut in a saucepan, pour the water over it, bring to the boil and simmer for 4–5 minutes. Allow to cool until hand-hot, then sieve and strain as described above.

Storing and using coconut milk Coconut milk can be stored in the fridge for a day or so but it does not keep and must be used while fresh. It will not freeze: if you are cooking for the freezer, leave out the coconut milk and add it when the dish has been thawed ready for final reheating. (An exception in this book is Rendang, where the coconut milk is almost totally absorbed by the meat during the long cooking process. Rendang freezes very successfully.)

Coconut cream This is the thick white liquid that separates and gathers at the surface if you refrigerate coconut milk. A few recipes specify the cream, and you simply spoon it off as required. If you want the milk, however, just stir the 'cream' back into the clearer liquid on which it floats.

Creamed coconut The creamed coconut that you can buy in blocks is fine if the recipe asks for coconut milk to be added just before the dish is served, but it should not be used during cooking – it curdles. It is a convenient way of thickening a sauce that turns out at the last moment to be thinner than it should be. Cut off the amount you need from the block, then dilute it with a little hot water before adding it to your dish.

Coriander leaves and roots (*Coriandrum sativum*)

Indonesians use only the seeds, but in Thailand they use the leaves and stalks and the roots as well. For-tunately it is becoming easier to buy fresh coriander in England. Unfortunately the long roots are often cut off because it is assumed the plant 'looks better' with-out them; but in any trayful, a few will have a reason-able amount of root left on. Roots can be frozen – leave a short piece of stem on each root before wrapping for the freezer.

Coriander seeds, cumin seeds

A few recipes call for these seeds to be roasted. Roast them either in a moderate oven or on the stove. Spread a small quantity of the seeds in an ovenproof dish or a frying pan and heat for a few minutes, shaking the pan or dish several times as if you were roasting almonds. When the seeds are ready, they will have darkened somewhat and there will be a strong, pleasant aroma.

Fermented yellow or black beans

Indonesian, *tauco* – which is really the Chinese word.

These are used in dishes of Chinese origin, and are easy to find, tinned, in Chinese shops. For the black fermented beans, the dried ones packed in small boxes or wrapped in plastic bags are better than the tinned ones in brine.

Fish sauce

Thai, *nam pla*. This is a salty, savoury, appetite-whetting sauce which is used in a great many Thai dishes and has much the same function as soya sauce (*kecap*) in Indonesian cooking.

Flat-leaved parsley

This also known in England as 'Continental' parsley.

Galingale or galangal (*Languas galanga*)

Indonesian, *laos*; Thai, *ka*. This is a rhyzome or root, rather like ginger but with a somewhat mellower taste. Fresh galingale, which is available in London occasionally, can be chopped like ginger, and the suggestions for the use of ginger (see below) apply to galingale as well. It is also available in dried form. If using a large piece of dried galingale remember to take it out before serving. Laos powder or galingale powder is also widely available.

Ginger (*Zingiber officinale*)

Many of these recipes specify root ginger, which used to be called 'green' ginger – if it is from a young plant, the roots often have a greenish tinge. If you like ginger, put plenty in, chop it fine and enjoy it. If you don't particularly want the individual gingery taste to come through, then simply cut the ginger into two or three thick slices, which should be easy to locate and remove before the dish is served. If you really don't like ginger or can't buy root ginger, use a little powdered ginger instead. It will make its own small contribution to the overall effect. Pickled ginger is also available in jars; it is very good and can be used instead of fresh ginger if need be.

Kaffir lime (*Citrus hystrix*)

Indonesian, *jeruk purut*; Thai, *makrut*. A type of citrus fruit found in many parts of South-East Asia but not easy to find in the West, except for the dried leaves and rinds, which can be bought in Asian shops. (Fresh leaves are obtainable in a few Thai shops in London and elsewhere.) The leaves (*daun jeruk purut, bai makrut*) are used in Indonesia and Thailand; the rind (*piw makrut*) in Thailand only.

Kecap manis: see Soya sauce

Lemon grass (*Cymbopogon citratus*)

Indonesian, *sereh*; Thai, *takrai*. This herb, which does look like a coarse, heavy type of grass, is used in many recipes for its mildly sour-sweet, citrusy flavour. It can be bought, fresh or ground, in many Asian shops, or may sometimes be persuaded to grow as a house plant. It is sold in stems about 6 in (15 cm) long, with the tough but fragrant outer leaves trimmed short. For most dishes, cut the stem into 3 equal lengths; one of these pieces is usually sufficient. Remember to remove it before serving. For Thai curries and the Balinese 'bumbu lengkap', the outer leaves are stripped off and only the tender heart is used, chopped into rounds like a spring onion or put together with other spices to be blended into a smooth paste.

Mustard greens

You can buy these fresh in many Chinese shops; there are several slightly-differing varieties. They are not 'Chinese leaves' (which nowadays are stocked by many supermarkets as well as by your neighbourhood greengrocer), but Chinese leaves are a perfectly acceptable substitute. You can also get them in cans, canned in Bangkok and called Green Mustard Pickles. The cans are conveniently small; the drained weight is usually 3½ oz (100 g). There are also larger cans (20 oz/567 g), packed in China, labelled Salted Mustard Greens; these are just the same thing, and very good.

Noodles

Indonesian and Thai, *mie* or *mee* (from Chinese). There are many types, just as there are of pasta. Here are the ones you are most likely to come across.

Egg noodles (*bakmie, ba mee*)   these look very like spaghetti, except they are usually sold in tangled yellow blocks, not bunches of straight sticks. You can occasionally buy fresh ones in Chinese shops in London, but the dried ones in packets are really just as good and will keep for months. There are round ones and flat ones.

Rice vermicelli (*miehun, sen mee*)   very thin, sold in what looks like a skein of whitish wire. A thicker type are rice noodles and are labelled 'rice sticks' – these are like bundles of narrow white ribbon.

Bean threads (*biehun, woon sen*)   also called cellophane noodles, because they are colourless and almost transparent. These are also very thin. They are made from mung beans.

Palm sugar

(Indonesian, *gula jawa, gula merah* or *gula melaka*; Thai, *nam tan peep*). This is a brown sugar made from the juice of the coconut palm flower; it is sold in hard cakes, and you grate it, scrape it or hack a piece off and crush it. Some shops may call it by its Anglo-Burmese name, jaggery.

Pandanus (*Pandanus odorus, P. odoratissimus*)

Indonesian, *pandan* (*daun pandan* is the leaf, which is the part used in cooking); Thai, *bai toey hom*. Packets of fresh pandanus leaves are now fairly easy to find in large British towns. They are also called screwpine leaves. They are used for colouring and flavouring.

Pea aubergines

These are tiny, spherical aubergines which really are about the size of large peas. Indonesians generally eat them raw (they are good with sambal) but they can equally well be cooked. The Thais use them in curries.

Peanuts   (*Arachis hypogaea*)

Indonesian, *kacang tanah*; Thai, *tooa*. Use raw, unsalted peanuts, which are easy enough to obtain in most areas. They are used in South-East Asia because they are cheap, filling and nutritious. Like chillies, peanuts or groundnuts were brought from Central America by Columbus and co. Today, you wonder how Asia ever managed without them. The use of peanut butter as a short cut to saté sauce is not recommended, but it is possible.

Rice

As an Indonesian, I have to say that the best rice available in the west for the purposes of Indonesian and Thai cookery is 'Thai fragrant' rice – there are several brands on sale in London and elsewhere. Although it may be described as 'perfumed' on the bag, the only fragrance is a very pleasant smell of freshly-cooked rice that issues from the kitchen at dinner time. I always cook my rice in an electric steamer, using 1¼ cups of water to every cup of dry rice; this gives the rather moist, slightly sticky boiled rice that Indonesians like. If you prefer harder, separate grains, you can use a little less water or go for Basmati or some other type.

Glutinous or 'sticky' rice is used in Indonesia for making sweets, but it is also eaten as a staple main-course food and is well worth trying. It is more filling than ordinary long-grain, so don't cook quite as much as you normally would. Most short-grain rice is rather sweet and one variety is used mainly (by the English anyway) for rice pudding, though some Japanese savoury rice is short-grained. There is nothing wrong with processed or boil-in-the-bag or instant rice, except that it is more expensive and, to my mind, a bit bland.

If you don't have an electric rice cooker, rice is still very easy to boil: wash it well, and put it in a heavy saucepan with about its own volume of water. Don't put any salt in at any time. Bring the water to the boil, then simmer quietly, uncovered, until the rice has absorbed it all. Then cover the pan – even weigh the lid down if you conveniently can – and continue cooking on a low heat for 10 minutes. The layer of rice that sticks to the bottom should be thrown away (unless you like to take it out, dry it thoroughly, and then deep-fry it, as Indonesians do). If you have a double-saucepan steamer, steam the rice in it for the final 10 minutes (but note that steamed rice needs to absorb more water in the first stage of cooking – up to 1½ times its own volume).

Rice that is to be fried needs to be boiled as described above, but in a little less water; it should then be left to cool – not overnight, but at least for a couple of hours. If you don't do this, the fried rice will be eatable but rather soggy.

Salam leaf (*Eugenia polyantha*)

(Indonesian, *daun salam*) A single salam leaf is placed in the pan during cooking. Dried leaves are sold in most Oriental foodstores, but a bay leaf is a good substitute.

Sambal

This is the Indonesian word for hot chilli relish, which is used both in cooking and as a condiment. You can make your own, or buy it from most Asian food stores and many supermarkets. 'Basic' sambal (page 118) is simply crushed red chillies and salt, and is called sambal ulek (spelled *oelek* in Holland, where the 1972 spelling reform has not penetrated yet). But there is a whole repertoire of sambals to which other highly-flavoured ingredients have been added, e.g. sambal manis (sweet and relatively mild), sambal kemiri (with candlenuts), sambal udang (with prawns) etc.

Shrimps, dried

Indonesian, *ebi*. These very tiny dried shrimps are not hard to get, provided you have a Chinese or Malaysian or Thai store within reach, but they are surprisingly expensive. They are usually roasted before being packaged for sale. Soak in cold water for 10 minutes before use, then chop or put in a blender or crush with a pestle and mortar.

Shrimp paste

Indonesian, *terasi* (also spelled *trassie*; the names *balachan* and *blachen* are also used); Thai, *kapee* or *kapi*. This is an extremely pungent, salty, savoury hard paste which is used throughout Indonesia, Malaysia and Thailand, but only in very small amounts. If in doubt, use less rather than more. It is sold in blocks, and I usually slice the block or cut it up and put the pieces in an airtight jar for storage; it keeps almost indefinitely. For a few recipes, the paste is grilled or fried before use. (At least one Dutch distributor also sells it in packaged slices, ready-grilled.) The fried or grilled shrimp paste can be crumbled so it can be measured with a teaspoon. 'Raw' paste is crushed or blended along with other spices for dishes in which the spiced paste is then fried. Whatever you think of the smell (and some Westerners like it, when they get used to it), you will find it does great things for your savoury dishes, so do use it if you can find it – it is not rare nowadays, at least in England.

Som sa

Indonesian, *jeruk sambal*. These are very small green limes, even smaller than a kaffir lime. Available in Thai food stores, but ordinary limes can be used.

Soya sauce (or soy sauce)

(Indonesian, *kecap* – pronounced, of course, 'ketchup'). This dark-coloured, salty-tasting liquid has been produced from soya beans, by a complicated process of fermentation, for centuries. The familiar Amoy or Kikkoman, or any commercially-available brand, is perfectly good for any of the dishes in this book. Some recipes, however, specify light or dark soy, and there is a perceptible difference in taste. By and large, light soya sauce is thinner and saltier, dark is thicker and sweeter. All soya sauces are strong-tasting and must be used sparingly; even the darkest contains a lot of salt.

A commonly-sold brand (in the UK, at any rate) is Pearl River Bridge. This is a good, moderately-priced sauce, but the labelling is rather confusing. 'Soy Superior' is light; 'Superior Soy' is dark. The dark sauce also has the French word *épais* on the label.

Real Indonesian *kecap* is not easy to find, even in London, but one can do perfectly well without it. A few shops sell Javanese-style brands that are made in Holland. *Kecap manis* simply means 'sweet' (i.e. dark) soy.

Spring roll wrappers

These are thin pastry squares which are essential for making spring rolls. They can be bought, usually from the freezer, in Chinese food shops. They come in several sizes; I use 5 in (12½ cm) and 8½ in (22 cm) squares (50 and 20 sheets respectively, per packet). The pastry gets dry very easily, so the best way to work with it is to thaw the whole packet completely and peel the sheets off, very carefully, one by one; you can then freeze them again. Once they have been separated they can be filled and rolled quickly and easily.

Tamarind (*Tamarindus indica*)

Indonesian, *asam* or *assem*; Thai, *mak kam*. Important for giving dishes the faint sourness that counteracts and gives depth to the sweetness of much South-East Asian food. Many of my recipes specify tamarind water, which is made by simmering a chunk of dried tamarind pulp in water for several minutes, letting it cool and then squeezing and pressing it to extract the juices and flavour. Discard the remains of the pulp and put the dark-coloured, unappetising liquid in with the rest of the ingredients. It will taste good. If you use tamarind water often, it is worth making a small stock of it; it will keep in the fridge for at least a month. Put a whole 1 lb (500 g) block into 2 pints (1.2 l) of water and simmer till the liquid has reduced to half its volume. Then squeeze and sieve as before, and store the thick liquid in an airtight jar.

Chinese shops sell 'tamarind slices' which are really *asam gelugur* (*Garcinia atroviridis*) but can be used instead of tamarind water, remember to take them out before serving.

Tempeh

Tempeh (Indonesian *tempe*) is a block made from soya beans, cooked and then fermented with a special yeast or mould. This 'digests' the part of the soya bean that human beings cannot, so the full nutritional value of the beans is preserved and indeed enhanced. Tempeh looks a bit like cream cheese on the outside; when you slice it you can see the individual beans, knitted together (as it were) by the mould. It has a more interesting flavour and texture than tofu (beancurd; Indonesian *tahu*). It is becoming a well-known health food in North America, and is made by several small firms in England. Some health food shops import frozen tempeh from Holland. Don't eat tempeh if it is so overripe that it smells of ammonia.

Tofu: see Beancurd

Water chestnuts

These are easily obtainable in tins from almost all Chinese food shops, and can sometimes be bought fresh.

Wonton wrappers

These are squares of very thin pastry, like lasagne but much thinner. They measure about 3 in (7½ cm) each way, and can be bought from any Chinese shop because they are necessary for making such Chinese delicacies as wonton soup. They must be bought either fresh or frozen; their life in the refrigerator is limited to a few days. If you freeze them, pack them in small packets (say, 4 oz or 100 g in a packet) and thaw them completely, peeling each one off the pile before use. Remember, though, that they dry out very quickly and become brittle. You *can* make your own 'wanton skins' (as my Chinese supplier labels them), in which case a pasta machine is a help. The ingredients are: 10 oz (300 g) plain flour, 2 eggs, salt, cold water. I doubt if it is really worth the trouble if you can buy them.

Woodears fungus

These are sold in Chinese shops, where they are often labelled 'dried black fungus'. At this stage they look neither appetising nor edible, but 30 minutes' soak in hot water makes them soft and they are delicious as part of the filling of a spring roll. Not cheap, but nowhere near as pricey as Chinese floral mushrooms.

SOUPS AND STARTERS

I sometimes have the feeling that the human race is divided into 'wet' and 'dry' eaters – but at other times I feel it must be more complicated than that. I've got used, anyway, to the idea of starting off a dinner party with soup, even though in Indonesia and Thailand soup would be on the table all the way through, to wash the food down. We do not drink wine; and my grandmother would not even let us drink water during a meal, because water and rice, she said, would make us feel uncomfortably full, and we were supposed to enjoy her superb cooking. What I have found works well for a dinner party is to start off with one, sometimes two, dishes which are 'dry' in the sense that they have little or no sauce. Only then do you have the soup, so that it forms a kind of first-act finale.

Among the soups, soto, laksa and tom yam gung can represent Indonesia, Malaysia and Thailand respectively. On the drier side, saté is familiar in all three countries, as are spring rolls in one shape or another, even though they were originally Chinese. What all these dishes have in common is the way they exploit contrasts of taste and texture – the crunchy skin of the spring roll against the spicy smoothness of the sauce, or the different sensations you get from crab and young sweet corn when you bite into them.

Soup tureen, whole tamarind, tamarind slices, galingale, kaffir lime leaves, lemon grass cut in rounds, yard-long beans

Tom Sum
Hot and sour soup with fish

Serves 4–6

FOR THE STOCK
2 pints (1.2 l) cold water
3 tamarind slices
2–4 fresh or dried chillies
2 kaffir lime leaves
1 in (2½ cm) root ginger
1 in (2½ cm) fresh or dried galingale
1 stalk fresh lemon grass, cut into three
½ tsp salt

1 tbs peanut or vegetable oil
1 medium-sized onion, chopped
1 pint (600 ml) strong clear chicken
    stock (optional)
4 oz (120 g) mustard greens
4 oz (120 g) watercress
1 small white radish (about
    4 oz/120 g), finely sliced
1 lb (450 g) white fish, cut into large
    pieces
3 tbs chopped coriander leaves
1 tbs light soya sauce
1 tbs fish sauce

For this soup choose any white fish without small bones. Angler fish or fillet of sole, or cod are all quite suitable. You can also mix several kinds of fish. Use whatever vegetables you like; I like green vegetables, such as Chinese mustard greens and watercress, mixed with white radish.

The stock should always be clear and transparent and the soup doesn't need to be too sour or too hot. The sourness comes from the tamarind, but I often use a very good chicken stock and put in the juice of one lemon just before serving. What follows, however, is the authentic way of making hot and sour soup.

Make sure there are no bones left in the fish.

Put the water into a large saucepan with the tamarind slices, chillies, kaffir lime leaves, ginger, galingale, lemon grass and salt. Bring to the boil and simmer for 20–30 minutes. By this time the stock will be very fragrant from the lemon grass and other aromatic ingredients. Strain this through a fine sieve, discarding the solids.

In a large saucepan, heat the oil and fry the chopped onion until soft, then add the stock you have just made. Simmer for 15 minutes. Add the chicken stock, if used, or 1 pint (600 ml) water or vegetable stock (this additional liquid is needed if the soup is to serve 6 people). Add the mustard greens, watercress and white radish. Simmer for 4 minutes. Increase the heat and bring the stock to a rolling boil, then add the fish and coriander leaf. Let the mixture boil for 4 minutes, and add the soya sauce and the fish sauce. Cook the soup for just 1 more minute, then serve immediately.

Tom Yam Gung
Hot and sour soup with prawns

Serves 4–6

1 lb (450 g) large prawns, with shells
1 tsp salt
2 pints (1.2 l) cold water
3 tamarind slices
2 kaffir lime leaves
2–4 fresh or dried chillies
1 in (2½ cm) root ginger
1 in (2½ cm) fresh or dried galingale
1 stalk fresh lemon grass, cut into three
1 tbs peanut or vegetable oil
1 medium-sized onion, chopped
1 pint (600 ml) strong clear chicken
  stock (optional)
2 medium-sized carrots
1 small white radish (about
  4 oz/120 g)
4 oz (120 g) mustard greens or
  watercress
2 oz (60 g) oyster mushrooms or 1 oz
  (30 g) woodear fungus
1 tbs fish sauce

This is the most popular of the Thai hot and sour soups. Of all those that I have eaten in Thai restaurants, the best had plenty of prawns and only a small quantity of vegetables. The vegetables, for choice, should be Chinese mustard greens and dried mushrooms. At my own dinner parties I normally use carrots and white radish, with a little mustard greens or watercress and Chinese dried mushrooms or, if I can get them, fresh oyster mushrooms.

The stock should always be clear and transparent; in a white porcelain soup bowl, the colours look pretty. The soup doesn't need to be too sour or too hot. The sourness should be from tamarind, but I often use a very good chicken stock and put in the juice of one lemon just before serving. What follows, however, is the authentic way of making hot and sour soup.

Peel and devein the prawns. Wash the prawns, and the shells, very thoroughly. Put the prawns on a plate, sprinkle with half the salt and keep in the fridge until needed. Put the shells aside.

Put the water into a large saucepan with the tamarind slices, chillies, kaffir lime leaves, ginger, galingale, lemon grass and the remaining salt. Bring this to the boil and simmer for 20–30 minutes. By this time the stock will be very fragrant from the lemon grass and other aromatic ingredients.

In a small saucepan, heat the oil and fry the chopped onion until soft, then add the prawn shells and stir for about 2 minutes. Put the onion and prawn shells, without any oil, into the stock pot. Continue to simmer for 15 minutes. Then strain the stock through a fine sieve, or a sieve lined with muslin, into another large saucepan. Discard the solids. Add the chicken stock, if used, or water or vegetable stock (this additional liquid is needed if the soup is to serve 6 people). Keep aside to reheat later.

While the hot and sour stock is brewing, prepare the vegetables. Peel the carrots and white radish and cut them into thin rounds. If the white radish is very large, cut the rounds in half. Pick over and wash the mustard greens or watercress. Shred the oyster mushrooms. If using dried mushrooms, soak these in boiling water for 30 minutes, then remove the stalks; put the stalks and the water into the stock pot. Slice the mushrooms, which are now quite soft.

Put the clear and strained stock to boil gently. Add the carrots and white radish and mushrooms. Simmer for 10 minutes. Increase the heat and bring the stock to a rolling boil, then add the prawns. Let the mixture boil for 3 minutes, and add the mustard greens or watercress and the fish sauce. Cook the soup for just *one* more minute, then serve immediately.

Sup Kepiting Dengan Jagung Muda

Crabmeat and baby corn soup

Serves 4–6

1 tbs sunflower oil
6 shallots, thinly sliced
1 tbs sugar
8 oz (225 g) baby sweet corn, thinly sliced
a pinch of chilli powder
3 large slices root ginger
salt to taste
2 tsp light soya sauce
1 pint (600 ml) good chicken stock
8 oz (225 g) crabmeat (white meat only); fresh, frozen or canned
4 oz (120 g) fried tofu, thinly sliced
3 tbs roughly chopped flat-leaved parsley
3 tbs thinly sliced spring onions or chives

I developed this soup at the Inter-Continental Hotel in London from a very simple everyday recipe that we had often at home when I was young. It is a sweet soup, which is very refreshing, especially as in Indonesia we eat soup all the way through an otherwise rather spicy meal.

In a saucepan heat the oil, fry the shallots for 2 minutes, add the sugar and stir continuously for another 2 minutes. Add the baby corn, stir and add the chilli powder, ginger, salt and soya sauce. Add the stock, then bring to the boil and simmer for 25–30 minutes. Taste, add more salt if necessary.

Stir in the crab meat, tofu, chopped parsley and spring onions and simmer for 3–5 minutes. Discard the ginger slices before serving hot.

Laksa Lemak
Prawn and vermicelli soup

Serves 4–6

4 oz (120 g) pork fillet or chicken
   breast
6 oz (175 g) prawns, with shells
6 oz (175 g) rice vermicelli
1 pint (600 ml) water
1¹/₂ tsp vegetable oil
5 shallots, thinly sliced
2 cloves garlic, crushed
2 in (5 cm) root ginger
1 tsp ground coriander
¹/₂ tsp turmeric
¹/₂ pint (300 ml) thick coconut milk
4 fried bean curds, thickly sliced (total
   weight about 4oz/120 g)
3 oz (85 g) beansprouts
salt and pepper to taste

FOR THE GARNISH
4–5 spring onions, thinly sliced

Laksa Lemak is really the Malaysian name for soto (soup) made with noodles and coconut milk. The Indonesians have adopted the name because an explanatory name in Indonesian would be very long. You will certainly find Laksa Lemak on restaurant menus in Malaysia and Singapore as well as Indonesia.

Boil the pork or chicken, seasoned with salt and pepper, in the water for 45 minutes. Drain the meat, reserving the stock, and slice into small, thin pieces. Clean the prawns and discard the heads.

Put the vermicelli into a saucepan and pour over enough boiling water to cover. Leave the pan covered for 5 minutes and then strain off the water.

Heat the oil in a wok or a deep saucepan, and sauté the sliced shallots for 1 minute. Add the crushed garlic, ginger, coriander and turmeric. Stir for another half-minute, then add the meat. Stir for 1 minute more, add the stock and simmer for 25 minutes.

Add the vermicelli and the coconut milk and let everything continue to simmer very gently. When the coconut milk starts to boil, stir gently to prevent it from curdling.

Add the prawns, bean curds and beansprouts and simmer for another 5 minutes, stirring occasionally. Just before serving, add the spring onions. Serve hot.

Soto Madura
Madura beef soup

Serves 6–8 as a starter

1 lb (450 g) boned brisket of beef,
   trimmed
2¹/₂ pints (1¹/₂ l) water
salt to taste
freshly ground black pepper
2 tbs corn oil
4 candlenuts, chopped
1 onion, chopped
3 cloves garlic, chopped
3 oz (85 g) prawns, with shells,
   roughly chopped
1 in (2¹/₂ cm) root ginger
¹/₄ tsp turmeric powder
3 shallots, finely chopped
¹/₂ tsp chilli powder (optional)

FOR THE GARNISH
2 oz (60 g) beansprouts (optional)
1 tbs flat-leaved parsley
1 tbs fried shallots or onion (page 120)
4 lemon slices

This is quite a widely known dish, but many people evidently think that it should be made with chicken. There certainly are other kinds of soto that use chicken, but Soto Madura should have beef; after all, the island from which it takes its name is famous for its buffaloes. It is equally good as part of an elaborate party meal or by itself.

Put the beef into a large saucepan, cover with the water, add a little salt and pepper. Bring to the boil, cover and simmer for 1 hour 15 minutes, skimming all the time.

Remove the meat from the pan, and strain the stock through a fine sieve into a bowl. Keep aside. Cut the meat into small cubes, discarding any fat or gristle.

Heat 1 tablespoonful of oil in a saucepan, and fry the chopped ingredients for 1 minute. Add the ginger, turmeric and half the meat stock. Cover and simmer for 15 minutes.

Fry the chopped shallots in a large pan until they are golden brown, using the remaining oil. Add the beef, 4 tablespoons of the stock, a little salt and the chilli powder (if desired). Cover and simmer for 2 minutes.

Strain the liquid in which the prawns and candlenuts were cooked into the pan that contains the beef. Put in the rest of the stock. Bring to the boil, lower the heat, cover and simmer for 20–25 minutes. If beansprouts are used put them in just before serving hot, garnished with parsley, fried shallots and lemon slices.

Popia Tawt
Fried miniature spring rolls

Makes 50 spring rolls

1 packet of 50 spring roll wrappers
  (5 in/12½ cm square)

FOR THE STUFFING
3½ oz (100 g) packet cellophane
  noodles
8 oz (225 g) uncooked prawns, without shells
4 oz (120 g) crabmeat (white meat
  only)
4 carrots, cut into tiny matchsticks
4 oz (120 g) white cabbage, shredded
½ oz (15 g) woodears fungus, soaked
  in hot water for 4 minutes, rinsed
  and chopped
5 spring onions, thinly sliced
2 cloves of garlic, crushed
½ in (1 cm) root ginger, finely chopped
½ tsp chilli powder
1 tsp salt
1 tbs light soya sauce

1 egg
vegetable oil for frying
crispy lettuce leaves
sweet and sour chilli sauce (page 124)

Miniature spring rolls are normally served as a starter in Thai restaurants. They are similar to Indonesian lumpia, *though not as big. I myself have served them hundreds of times as finger food at drinks parties, or as a first course. I admit that, although I always make the filling, the job of rolling them I delegate to a Philippine girl friend of mine who makes all the rolls exactly the same size and perfect. You can vary the filling, using prawns with pork, chicken or crab meat, or you can have a vegetable filling. Here is my favourite, prawn and crabmeat, using the white meat only.*

These ingredients will make about 50 miniature spring rolls. The wrappers can be bought in oriental supermarkets, usually from the freezer (see page 21).

Assuming the wrappers are bought frozen, thaw them out completely and carefully peel each one from the pile. Then cover them with a tea towel to prevent them from drying.

Soak the cellophane noodles in hot water for 3 minutes, drain and roughly chop. In a large bowl mix together the stuffing ingredients. Separate the egg, mix the yolk thoroughly into the filling, and save the white in a bowl (you will need it for sealing the rolls).

Put a wrapper on a flat surface (e.g. a plate or tray); put about 2 teaspoons of the filling onto the corner nearest you. Pull the corner over the filling and roll up the wrapper with the filling inside it, but leave the corner furthest from you free, like the flap of an envelope. Then fold the two side flaps towards the centre, brush the remaining flap with egg white and fold it so that the roll is sealed. Repeat the process until all the rolls are made and sealed.

Deep-fry the rolls, 6 or 8 at a time, in hot oil until golden brown and crisp. Serve hot with crispy lettuce leaves and sweet and sour chilli sauce. To eat, wrap each one in a lettuce leaf, then dip it into the sauce.

Popia Soht
Steamed spring rolls

Makes about 20 spring rolls

2 oz (60 g) packet of cellophane
    noodles
1/2 oz (15 g) woodears fungus
2 tbs vegetable oil
1 lb (450 g) carrots, cut into tiny
    matchsticks
8 oz (225 g) French beans, cut into
    thin rounds
4 oz (120 g) white cabbage, very finely
    shredded
6 oz (170 g) canned bamboo shoots,
    cut into tiny matchsticks
1 tsp salt
1/2 tsp ground white pepper
5 spring onions, thinly sliced
1/2 in (1 cm) root ginger, chopped
2 tbs light soya sauce
1 egg, separated
1 packet of 20 spring roll wrappers
    (8 1/2 in/22 cm square)

These spring rolls are normally filled with minced pork, prawns, bamboo shoots and beansprouts. However, for steamed spring rolls, I prefer a vegetarian version: after all, they are called 'spring' rolls because originally they were filled with spring vegetables. Like the miniature fried spring rolls, these are served in Thai restaurants as a starter.

Soak the cellophane noodles in hot water for 5 minutes, drain and cut up roughly. Soak the woodears fungus in hot water for 4 minutes, rinse and chop.

Heat the oil in a wok or frying pan and start stir-frying the vegetables: carrots first, then beans, cabbage and bamboo shoots. Season with the salt and pepper.

After 4 minutes of stir-frying, add the chopped cellophane noodles, woodears, spring onions and soya sauce. Continue stirring for another 2 minutes. Taste, and adjust the seasoning. Leave to cool. When cool, mix the egg yolk thoroughly into the filling, and save the white in a bowl (you will need it for sealing the rolls).

Now you can start rolling your spring rolls. Put a wrapper on a flat surface (e.g. a plate or tray); put about 2 tbs of the filling onto one corner. Pull the corner over the filling and roll up the wrapper with the filling inside it. Then fold the two side flaps towards the centre, brush the remaining flap with egg white and fold it up so that the roll is sealed. Repeat the process until all the rolls are made and sealed. Arrange in a single layer on a plate and steam the spring rolls for 4–5 minutes. Serve hot as a starter with Nam Chim (Sweet and Sour Chilli Sauce, page 124).

Saté Lilit

Minced pork saté Balinese style

Makes 12–16 saté

FOR THE SPICE MIXTURE
4 shallots
2 cloves garlic
5 red chillies, seeded, or 1 tsp chilli
 powder
2 candlenuts or 5 tbs very thick
 coconut milk
3 tsp coriander seeds
2 tsp cumin seeds
2 cloves
1 cinnamon stick, about 2 in (5 cm)
 long
½ tsp ground nutmeg
½ tsp ground turmeric
½ tsp ground galingale
½ tsp white pepper
2 in (5 cm) stalk of lemon grass or ½
 tsp lemon grass powder
a thin slice of shrimp paste about 2 in
 (5 cm) square (optional)
2 tbs vegetable oil
2 tbs water

2 tbs vegetable oil
1 tbs salt
1 lb (450 g) minced pork
juice of 1 lime
12–16 × 6 in (15 cm) bamboo saté
 sticks

Don't be put off by the long list of spices. The result is well worth the trouble of getting them all together. The Balinese call this combination of spices bumbu lengkap *(a complete set of spices); it is also used for Ayam Betutu (page 70) and Saté Bebek (page 31).*

Put all the ingredients for the spice mixture into a food processor and process until smooth. (Use a pestle and mortar if you prefer.) Fry this paste in the remaining 2 tbs oil, stirring continuously, for about 5 minutes or until the smell of raw shallots and garlic has been replaced by a pleasant spicy fragrance. Add the salt, and leave to cool.

When the paste is cool, mix it in a bowl with the minced pork. Knead with your hand for a while, then add the lime juice and mix again. Cover and chill for 1–2 hours.

Divide the meat mixture into 12–16 portions. Form each portion into a ball, then put the saté stick in the middle and with your hand form the meatball into a small sausage shape around the stick. Repeat this process until you have 12–16 sticks of saté.

Line the grill pan with aluminium foil, then grill the saté sticks, or cook on a charcoal barbecue, turning over carefully several times. Alternatively, cook in the oven at 180° C/350° F/Gas Mark 4 for 30–35 minutes, turning them once.

Serve hot as a snack lunch with a salad of your own choice or as a first course. They are also good for drinks parties, and as they are already quite spicy no other sauce will be necessary.

Saté Bebek
Duck saté Balinese style

Serves 4

4 pairs of fillets of duck breast
1 tbs salt
juice of 1 lime
8 × 8 in (20 cm) bamboo saté sticks

FOR THE SPICE MIXTURE
4 shallots, roughly chopped
2 cloves garlic, peeled
5 red chillies, seeded, or 1 tsp chilli
   powder
2 candlenuts or 5 tbs very thick
   coconut milk
3 tsp coriander seeds
2 tsp cumin seeds
2 cloves
1 cinnamon stick, about 2 in (5 cm)
   long
1/2 tsp ground nutmeg
1/2 tsp ground turmeric
1/2 tsp ground galingale
1/2 tsp white pepper
2 in (5 cm) lemon grass stalk or 1/2 tsp
   ground lemon grass
a thin slice of shrimp paste about 2 in
   (5 cm) square (optional)
1 tbs salt
2 tbs vegetable oil
2 tbs water

2 tbs vegetable oil for frying the paste

As with Saté Lilit (page 30), the marinade is the Balinese bumbu lengkap. From experience I can recommend this duck saté with no hesitation. It will be a hit any time. It is quite expensive to make, however, because the easiest way is to use the fillet of duck breast only.

Cut each duck breast into 4 pieces, leaving the skin which will be nice and crispy when cooked. Rub the pieces of duck with 1 tbs salt and the lime juice. Keep aside while preparing the spices.

Put all the ingredients for the spice mixture into a food processor and process until smooth. (Use a pestle and mortar if you prefer). Fry this paste in the remaining 2 tbs of oil, stirring continuously, for about 5 minutes or until the smell of raw shallots and garlic has been replaced by a pleasant spicy fragrance. Add the salt, and leave to cool.

When the paste is cool, mix it thoroughly with the duck. Then put 4 pieces of meat onto each bamboo stick, and leave to marinate for at least 2 hours or in the fridge overnight.

Grill the saté under a gas or electric grill or on a charcoal barbecue, for 10–12 minutes, turning several times, making sure that the skin is cooked longest so that it is crisp. Duck saté can also be cooked in the oven 200° C/400° F/Gas Mark 6 for 30–35 minutes, skin-side up.

Serve hot as a snack lunch with a salad of your own choice or as a first course. Also good for drinks parties, serving each piece of meat on a cocktail stick. As they are already quite spicy, no other sauce will be necessary.

Pepes Jamur
Spicy mushroom cups

Serves 4

*1 lb (450 g) mushrooms, sliced
salt
4 fl oz (120 ml) coconut cream
    (see p. 16)
2 green chillies, seeded
2 shallots, finely sliced
2 tbs chopped chives
2 tbs chopped mint
1 egg*

On a recent visit to Yogyakarta I think I ate this dish almost every day. It was usually made with jamur merang – *straw mushrooms – which people grow themselves or buy cheaply in the marketplace. The canned straw mushrooms that are available in the West are fine, but fresh mushrooms are the best, either cultivated or wild; the species is not important, as long as the mushrooms are safe to eat.*

Spread the sliced mushrooms on a plate and sprinkle with ½ teaspoon of salt.

Mix the coconut cream with all the other ingredients. Taste and add salt if desired, not forgetting that the mushrooms are already sprinkled with salt.

In Indonesia this mixture would then be wrapped in banana leaves and steamed for 10 minutes, to be eaten hot or cold as a snack. The easiest alternative method is to divide the mushroom mixture among 4 cups or ramekins, then steam; or cook in the oven at 180° C/350° F/Gas Mark 4 in a bain-marie for 10–15 minutes. Serve as a first course with thin slices of bread and butter or buttered toast, or just by itself.

Khai Kwan
Eggs stuffed with prawns and crabmeat

Serves 4 as a first course

4 large hen eggs, hard boiled
4 large uncooked prawns, without
  shells
4 tbs cooked crabmeat
1 tbs coriander leaves, chopped
2 cloves garlic, chopped
freshly ground black pepper
$^{1}/_{2}$ tsp salt
1 tbs fish sauce
4–5 tbs thick coconut milk

FOR THE BATTER
3 oz (85 g) plain flour
6 fl oz (170 ml) warm water
1 tbs vegetable oil
$^{1}/_{4}$ tsp salt
oil for deep frying

The real meaning of Khai Kwan is 'precious egg' or 'gift egg'. Khai Kwan can be eaten hot or cold as a first course with green salad. They can also be served with drinks before the meal, cut into 4 pieces with a sharp knife that has been wetted under the hot tap. If you have plenty of time, try making them with quail eggs – then they are even more precious.

Peel and halve the eggs. Scrape out the yolks and put them in a bowl.

Chop or mince the prawns and mix with them all the other ingredients except the coconut milk and the eggs. Add this mixture to the yolks in the bowl, mixing and mashing them with a fork. Add the coconut milk, a spoonful at a time, until the mixture is well blended and moist. You may find you need less than 5 tbs of coconut milk.

Divide the filling into 8 equal portions and put each portion into the half of an egg white, piling up the filling and shaping it so that you end up with 8 stuffed eggs.

To make the batter, put the flour, water, oil and salt in a bowl, and beat until smooth.

Dip each of the stuffed eggs in the batter and deep-fry in hot oil (180° C/350° F) for about 3 minutes or until golden brown, keeping the filling downwards while frying. Take each egg out with a slotted spoon and drain on kitchen paper.

Cumi-Cumi Isi
Stuffed squid

Serves 6–8

2 lb (1 kg) medium-sized squid
5 shallots or 1 onion, finely chopped
3 cloves garlic, finely chopped
1 large potato
4 carrots
1 tsp ground coriander
½ tsp chilli powder
½ in (1 cm) root ginger, finely chopped
1 tsp salt
2 large eggs
2 tbs oil
¼ pint (140 ml) water
2 tbs chopped flat-leaved parsley
4 tbs chopped spring onions
¼ pint (140 ml) tamarind water,
    seasoned with salt and pepper

Both the Indonesians and the Thais love squid; this one is an Indonesian squid recipe, which normally has a chilli-hot stuffing. But it is also good without chilli.

Clean the squid thoroughly, discarding the ink sacs. Chop the tentacles to mix with the stuffing. Cut the potato and carrots into very small cubes (less than ¼ in/ 5 mm). Keep the potato cubes in salted water to prevent discolouring.

In a wok or a shallow saucepan, heat the oil. Fry the chopped shallots (or onion) and garlic until soft, and add the carrots. Stir, then add the chopped ginger, ground coriander, chilli powder and salt. Stir almost continuously for about 3 minutes. Drain the potato, stir in, then add the water. Cover and simmer for 3 minutes.

Uncover, add the chopped tentacles and continue cooking for another 3 minutes, stirring frequently. Taste; add salt if necessary. When the vegetables are soft, remove the pan from the heat and allow to cool. Beat in the eggs, mixing thoroughly.

Use this mixture to stuff the squid, but don't fill each squid too full. Close the opening with wooden cocktail sticks. Arrange the squid in a heatproof dish, which should fit inside your steamer. (Alternatively, the squid may be cooked in the oven.) Sprinkle the chopped spring onions over the squid and pour on the seasoned tamarind water. Put the dish into the steamer and steam for 1 hour (or cook in a medium oven for the same time).

There will be quite a lot of juice in the dish when you finish steaming. Pour this sauce into a small saucepan, boil to reduce by half.

Leave to cool a little before removing the cocktail sticks and slicing the squid. Serve hot, with the sauce poured over, or cold.

RIGHT: *Sup Kepiting Dengan Jagung Muda/Crabmeat and Baby Corn Soup* (page 25)

Tiram Kukus
Spicy steamed scallops

Serves 4

*8 scallops with corals
1 clove garlic, crushed
1 green chilli, seeded and finely
   chopped
1 small piece ginger, finely chopped
1 tbs vegetable oil
a pinch of ground coriander
2 tbs light soya sauce
2 tbs water
1 tbs chopped chives*

You can steam the scallops in the shells or in little dishes or ramekins. I like my scallops quite spicy but plain, garnished with just a few chopped chives.

Clean the scallops and put 2 on each shell or dish.

Fry the garlic, chilli and ginger in the oil, stirring continuously, for 1 minute. Add the ground coriander, soya sauce and water. Simmer for 2 minutes. Strain, and discard the chopped ginger and chilli. Spoon this spiced liquid equally on to the scallops. Sprinkle each dish of scallops with chives, and steam for 3–4 minutes. Serve immediately.

LEFT: *Udang Nenas/Prawns with Pineapple (page 40) and Kembu Paria/ Stuffed Bitter Cucumber (page 94)*

FISH AND SHELLFISH

Indonesians sometimes refer to their country simply as *tanah air* – land and water. Less picturesquely, anyone who has ever been caught in a tropical downpour in Jakarta or Bangkok when there are no taxis in sight will appreciate how much water can fall from the sky in a few minutes. Indonesia, with its 13,000 islands, has an enormously long coastline.

Thailand is a more landlocked country, but it is seamed and threaded by networks of rivers. Both countries depend on wet rice cultivation for their staple food supply, so that irrigation systems, canals, reservoirs and storage tanks are part of the landscape almost everywhere you go. With so much water, fresh and salt, it would be astonishing if Thais and Indonesians were anything less than great fish cooks. Fortunately, most of our favourite fish, or very acceptable substitutes, can be found easily in British, American and Australian shops.

Thai boats in fish market

Sambal Goreng Tiram Dan Telur Puyuh

Scallop and quail egg sambal goreng

Serves 4

FOR THE SAUCE

4 shallots
1 clove garlic
3 large red chillies, seeded, or a pinch
  of chilli powder and 1 tsp paprika
2 candlenuts (optional)
$1/2$ in (1 cm) slice of shrimp paste
1 in ($2^{1/2}$ cm) root ginger
2 tbs olive oil
2 tbs water
1 tsp ground coriander
pinch of galingale powder
2 tbs olive oil for frying
1 tbs tamarind water or 1 tamarind
  slice
$1/2$–$3/4$ pint (300–450 ml) thick
  coconut milk
$1/2$ stalk lemon grass or a pinch of
  lemon grass powder
2 kaffir lime leaves or bay leaves
salt to taste

8 scallops, cleaned, with corals
  separated
12 quail eggs, boiled for 3 minutes and
  peeled
1 red tomato, peeled, seeded and
  chopped

'Sambal goreng' is a generic name for dishes that are found all over Indonesia. The best known is Sambal Goreng Udang (Prawn Sambal Goreng). However, this combination of scallops and quail eggs was suggested by one of my dinner-party guests at a celebration dinner at my home in Wimbledon. The dish turned out so well that I have made it many times since. We don't eat many scallops in Indonesia; when big restaurants and hotels use them they actually call them scallops, because the Indonesian name tiram includes mussels and oysters as well. Very few people called them by what I believe is their right name, kipas-kipas. I would just like to remind you that scallops need very little cooking, so put them into the sauce not more than 4 minutes before serving. Eat straight away and do not reheat.

Put the shallots, garlic, chillies, candlenuts (if used), shrimp paste, root ginger, oil and water in a blender, and blend until smooth. Add the ground coriander and galingale powder to this paste.

Put the olive oil in a saucepan, heat, and fry the paste from the blender, stirring continually, for 2 minutes. Add the tamarind water or tamarind slices, stir and add the coconut milk, lemon grass and kaffir lime leaves or bay leaves. Bring to the boil, then lower the heat and simmer, stirring frequently, for 50 minutes or until the sauce becomes as thick as you like it to be.

Adjust the seasoning. Take out the tamarind slice, if used, and lemon grass. Up to this point, you can prepare everything well in advance. Just before you are ready to serve, heat the sauce to a rolling boil, add the scallops and corals, quail eggs and tomatoes. Let this bubble gently for not longer than 4 minutes. Serve hot straight away.

Orak-Arik Kepiting
Stir-fried crab with egg

Serves 4

2 tbs coconut oil or peanut oil
4 shallots, finely chopped
1 in (2½ cm) root ginger, finely
  chopped
2 cloves garlic, finely chopped
8–10 oz (225–280 g) carrots or
  celeriac, grated or cut into fine
  julienne sticks
8 oz (225 g) crabmeat (white meat
  only)
1 tbs light soya sauce
2 duck or hen eggs, beaten
½ tsp ground coriander
a pinch of chilli powder
salt to taste
3 tbs chopped flat-leaved parsley or
  chives

This is a simple but very enjoyable dish that my mother cooked one day when I was still a high school student. I remember the day well – it was a rainy Sunday. My father, whose hobby was cooking, came back from market with several live crabs. One of them tried to escape into the courtyard outside our kitchen, which was half-flooded by the rain. I caught it and gave it to my father, with my eyes closed because I hated to watch the live crabs being plunged into the big saucepan of boiling water. However, I forgot this soon enough when the dish my father cooked was put on the table. It was quite out of this world – and its name has gone completely from my memory. It was much too complicated for a 14-year-old girl who hadn't the slightest interest in cooking.

This, then, is what my mother made later, from the left-over white meat of the crabs – and very good it is too.

In a wok or large frying pan, heat the oil. Fry the shallots, ginger and garlic for 2 minutes, stirring continuously. Add the carrots or celeriac and continue to stir-fry for 3–4 minutes or until the vegetables are tender. Then add the crabmeat and the soya sauce, and stir again for a minute or so.

Season the beaten eggs with the ground coriander, chilli powder and salt and add to the pan. Keep stirring and turning the mixture until the scrambled egg is well mixed with the crab and the vegetables. Stir in the chopped parsley or chives just before serving hot, to accompany a main course of rice or noodles.

Priew Wan Gung
Prawns in sweet and sour sauce

1 lb (450 g) medium-sized uncooked
   prawns, shelled and headless
1 tsp salt
4 fl oz (120 ml) peanut oil

FOR THE SAUCE
1 medium-sized green pepper
   (optional)
2 red tomatoes
2 cloves garlic
1 in (2½ cm) root ginger
8 fl oz (250 ml) water
¼ tsp cornflour (optional)
2 shallots, finely sliced
1 pinch of chilli powder
1 tbs fish sauce
1 tbs light soya sauce
2 tsp rice vinegar
1 tbs caster sugar
2 tbs chopped coriander leaves
   (optional)
2 spring onions, thinly sliced
salt and sugar to taste

This is another popular Thai restaurant dish which is simple to make at home. Just for a change, I have substituted tomatoes for tamarind in the sauce, but of course you can use tamarind water instead if you prefer.

Wash the prawns thoroughly. Drain and pat dry with kitchen paper. Sprinkle with the salt. Cut the green pepper into julienne strips and blanch quickly in boiling water.

Put the tomatoes, garlic and ginger and water in a small saucepan. Boil vigorously for 4 minutes – the water will be much reduced by then. Pass the contents of the pan through a sieve into a bowl, crushing the tomatoes and the garlic, so that you end up with several tablespoonfuls of thickish, garlicky, gingery tomato sauce. Set this aside to cool. When cool, if you are using cornflour, put it into this sauce.

In a wok or frying pan, heat the oil and fry the prawns in 2 batches for 3 minutes each time. Remove with a slotted spoon to drain in a colander.

Discard the oil, except for about 1½ tbs. Heat this and fry the shallots until soft. Add the chilli powder, fish sauce, soya sauce, vinegar and sugar. Stir, and add the tomato sauce. Stir again, simmer for 1 minute, turn up the heat a bit and add the prawns and green pepper (if used).

Stir continuously for another minute and add the chopped coriander leaves and spring onions. Continue cooking and stirring for 1 minute longer. Taste, and add sugar and salt if required. Serve immediately.

Udang Nenas
Prawns with pineapple

Serves 4

16–20 large uncooked prawns, peeled
  and deveined
salt
1 medium-sized pineapple

FOR THE SAUCE
3 shallots
2 cloves garlic
4 candlenuts
1/2 in (1 cm) root ginger
olive oil
water
a pinch of chilli powder
1 tbs white malt vinegar
2 tsp granulated sugar
4 fl oz (120 ml) cold water
2 tbs roughly chopped mint

At home in Indonesia, this dish always brought the cook a great many compliments, probably because I took care to use the best and freshest prawns I could find. When I got to England, I included the recipe as part of my entry for a wine-and-food menu competition. Not being a great wine-drinker myself, I overlooked the fact that pineapple doesn't go well with fine wines, so I didn't win. But it goes extremely well with prawns.

Serve this as a starter by itself, followed by a sweet soup such as Sup Kepiting Dengan Jagung Muda/Crabmeat and Baby Corn Soup (page 25). You will be ready then to enjoy the wine with the next course.

Wash the prawns. Drain, pat dry with kitchen paper and sprinkle with 1 tsp salt.

Peel the pineapple, cutting the peel quite thick. Core, and discard the eyes. Then cut into small cubes. Put in a colander and sprinkle liberally with salt. Leave for 10 minutes, then rinse thoroughly under a cold tap to wash the salt away.

Blend the shallots, garlic, candlenuts and root ginger with 2 tsp olive oil and 2 tbs water until smooth. Put 2 tbs olive oil in a wok or large frying pan, heat, and fry the paste from the blender, stirring continuously, for 2 minutes. Add chilli powder, vinegar and sugar. Stir and add the cold water. Simmer for 3 minutes, then adjust the seasoning.

Bring the sauce to a rolling boil and add the prawns. Stir, and let it bubble gently for 3 minutes. Add the pineapple cubes and mint and continue cooking, stirring all the time, for not more than 2 minutes longer. Serve hot or cold.

Homok Talay
Mixed shellfish in rich coconut milk sauce

Serves 4

8 scallops, with the corals
8 large prawns, with heads
8–12 mussels
8 crab claws
2 large squid, without tentacles

FOR THE SAUCE
3 large red chillies, seeded and chopped
4 shallots, chopped
3 cloves garlic
1 in (2½ cm) root ginger
2 in (5 cm) lemon grass stalk, outer
    leaves discarded
1½ pints (900 ml) very thick coconut
    milk
3 green cardamom seeds
2 tbs tamarind water or 2 tamarind
    slices
2 fresh kaffir lime leaves
1 tsp salt
1 tsp sugar
a handful of mint leaves
a handful of basil leaves
2 tbs chopped coriander leaves
    (optional)

*I enjoyed Homok Talay recently at the Blue Elephant, the smart
Thai restaurant in West London, where the dish was served in a
small earthenware pot which kept the heat and aroma of the food.
The taste was exquisite, spicy and full of mint and sweet basil and
lemon grass – a taste I am familiar with, as it occurs quite a lot in my
own Indonesian cooking. Here is my version of this delicious hot pot.
All the sea delicacies need very little cooking, so put them into the
sauce just a few minutes before serving.*

Clean the scallops, separate the corals, and cut the white part
in half. Remove the legs from the prawns, wash thoroughly.
Scrub the mussels well under a cold tap, then boil in water for 1
minute; leave in the hot water for a few more minutes, then
rinse these open mussels under cold water to get rid of the sand
that might remain inside the shell. Cut the squid into bite-
sized pieces, wash, boil in water with a large pinch of salt for
5–6 minutes, then drain.

Put the chillies, shallots, garlic, ginger and lemon grass into a
blender, add 3 tablespoons of the coconut milk and blend until
you have a very smooth paste. Then put another 4 tablespoons
of the coconut milk into a saucepan. Heat, and when boiling
stir with a wooden spoon and add the paste from the blender.
Stir again and leave to simmer for 1–2 minutes.

Add the cardamom seeds, tamarind water or slices, kaffir lime
leaves, salt and sugar. Once again stir and add the rest of the
coconut milk. Continue cooking and let this sauce bubble
gently for 30–40 minutes, stirring frequently to prevent curdling, until reduced by half.

Add the seafood and mint, basil and coriander leaves (if used),
and continue cooking for 4–5 minutes. Taste, adjust seasoning, remove the cardamom seeds and kaffir lime leaves, and
serve immediately.

Pud Pla Muek
Fried squid and vegetables with fish sauce

Serves 4

FOR THE SQUID
1½ lb (700 g) small squid, with
  tentacles
2 tbs tamarind water, or juice of 1
  lime
1 tsp salt

FOR THE SAUCE AND
VEGETABLES
1 lb (450 g) mustard greens, or
  Chinese leaves and broccoli
½ in (1 cm) slice of pickled ginger
1 clove pickled garlic
a pinch of galingale powder
a pinch of lemon grass powder
a pinch of chilli powder
2 tbs fish sauce
1 tsp sugar
½ pint (300 ml) vegetable oil for
  frying
1 tbs chopped coriander leaves
2 green chillies, seeded and chopped
  (optional)
salt

A very popular dish in Thai restaurants, where chefs sometimes, in their desire to be authentic, use too much lemon grass and coriander leaf. The result is that you can scarcely taste anything else. I make it at home with a milder sauce, and the flavours are much subtler. The Thais are fond, too, of pickled garlic, which suits this dish very well.

Clean the squid thoroughly, discarding the head and ink sac. Chop the tentacles roughly and slice the squid into small strips about ½ in × 1 in (1 cm × 2 cm). Marinate these in the tamarind water or lime juice and salt for 40 minutes – 1 hour. Then drain and pat dry with kitchen paper.

Clean and prepare the vegetables. The mustard greens need only be roughly chopped, Chinese leaves should be shredded coarsely, broccoli needs only to have the hard stalk cut off. You may wish to blanch the broccoli first.

Chop the pickled ginger and garlic very finely indeed or mash them in a pestle and mortar. Add the galingale powder, lemon grass powder, chilli powder, fish sauce and sugar. Mix well.

In a wok or frying pan heat the oil, and when really hot fry the squid in 2 or 3 batches for 3–4 minutes each time. Remove with a slotted spoon to drain in a colander.

When all the squid is fried, discard almost all the oil, leaving the wok or frying pan only just oily. Heat again, and when smoke starts to rise put in, first, the coriander leaves and chopped chillies (if used), stirring well, then all the vegetables. Stir and turn vigorously for 2 minutes. Add salt, stir again, then add the fish sauce mixture and continue stirring while you put in the fried squid. Mix well, taste, adjust seasoning and serve immediately.

Yam Pla Muek
Squid salad

Serves 4

1½ lb (700 g) cooked squid

FOR THE DRESSING
juice of 2 limes
1 tbs fish sauce
1 tbs sugar
1 green chilli, seeded and finely
  chopped
½ in (1 cm) stalk of lemon grass, soft
  inner part only, finely chopped
1 clove garlic, crushed (optional)
1 tbs finely chopped coriander leaves or
  flat-leaved parsley

Prepare the squid as you would for Pud Pla Muek/Fried Squid and Vegetables with Fish Sauce (page 42). Alternatively, for this typical Thai salad, instead of frying the squid you can boil it, with a little salt, for a fairly long time – maybe as long as an hour or more. If you boil it for 4–5 minutes, the chances are you will get a tender squid; cooking it for 15–20 minutes will make it tough and rubbery. But if you cook it longer still – say an hour and a half – it goes tender again. Don't ask me why.

Mix the dressing well. Dress the squid about 1 hour before serving.

Ikan Asam Manis
Fried fish in tamarind sauce

Serves 4

4 red snappers, cleaned

FOR THE MARINADE
2 tbs white malt vinegar
2 cloves garlic, crushed
1 tsp salt
1 tsp ground coriander
1/2 tsp turmeric

FOR THE SAUCE
2 oz (60 g) tamarind pulp
16 fl oz (450 ml) water
2 in (5 cm) root ginger, chopped
2 cloves garlic, chopped
2 tsp brown sugar
1/2 tsp chilli powder
4 spring onions, thinly sliced
salt
2 tbs olive oil

FOR THE GARNISH
2 tbs sliced gherkins
2 tbs chopped basil or mint
oil for frying

For best results the sour and sweet sauce for this recipe should be made of tamarind water spiced with chilli, garlic and ginger.

Mix together the marinade ingredients. Rub all over the fish and marinate for 1 hour.

Meanwhile, make the sauce. Dissolve the tamarind pulp in the water, then sieve it. Boil the liquid in a small saucepan until the quantity is reduced by half. In a frying pan or a wok, heat the oil, sauté the ginger and garlic for a few seconds, add the sugar, chilli powder, salt and spring onions, and stir. Stir in the thick tamarind water and adjust the seasoning.

Fry the fish in hot oil for about 5 minutes each side, turning them over once. Put the fish on a serving dish, heat the sauce quickly and pour over the fish, garnished with sliced gherkins and basil or mint. Serve immediately.

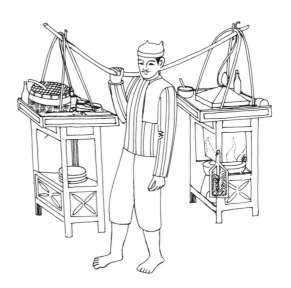

Ikan Kukus Dengan Mangga
Sea bass in sweet and sour sauce with mangoes

Serves 4–6

sea bass weighing 3–3¹/2 lb (about
   1¹/2 kg)
¹/2 tsp salt
juice of 1 lime
¹/2 stalk of lemon grass
3 fresh kaffir lime leaves
2 half-ripe mangoes
3 shallots
2 cloves of garlic (optional)
¹/2 in (1 cm) root ginger
3 candlenuts or macadamia nuts
1 tbs wine vinegar
2 tbs olive oil
¹/2 tsp turmeric powder
a pinch of chilli powder
1–2 tsp sugar
salt
4 fl oz (120 ml) water

Half-ripe mangoes are often used in salads and sauces – partly because mango trees grow in almost everyone's back yard. In any case, most Indonesian housewives, and their husbands, still enjoy cooking with their own home-grown fruit and vegetables, in spite of the fashion for imported foodstuffs. This dish will always make a big impression at any dinner party, whatever country you are in.

Clean, gut and scale the sea bass if your fishmonger hasn't done it for you. Rub the fish with salt and lime juice inside and out and place the lemon grass and kaffir lime leaves inside the fish.

Peel the mangoes, cut two good slices from each and cut these into julienne strips. Set aside for use later. With a sharp knife, cut all the remaining flesh from the mango stones, purée in a blender and set aside. Put the shallots, garlic if used, ginger, candlenuts or macadamia nuts, vinegar and half the olive oil into the blender and blend to a smooth paste.

Heat the remaining oil in a wok or frying pan and fry the puréed shallot mixture, stirring continuously, for 2 minutes. Then add the turmeric and chilli powder, stir, and add the mango purée, with sugar and salt to taste. Add the water and simmer gently for 5 minutes. Take the sauce off the stove, and keep it to be reheated just before serving.

Steam the fish for about 15–20 minutes and arrange it on a serving dish. Reheat the sauce, add the julienne of mangoes, stir, and simmer for 2 minutes. Pour the hot mango sauce over the fish, and serve immediately. In Indonesia, rice and vegetables would be the natural accompaniments, but this fish is equally good with pasta or new potatoes and salad.

Kare Ikan Dengan Lombok Hijau
Fish with green chilli in curry sauce

Serves 4–6

2 lb (1 kg) sea perch, filleted, cut into
   1 in (2½ cm) squares
1 tsp salt

FOR THE PASTE
5 shallots or 1 onion, chopped
3 cloves garlic, chopped
½ in (1 cm) root ginger, chopped
2 candlenuts (optional)
2 tbs olive oil
2 tbs water

½ pint (300 ml) thick coconut milk
4 large green chillies, seeded and cut
   diagonally
pinch of galingale powder
1 tsp ground coriander
1 tsp ground cumin
½ tsp turmeric powder
2 tbs tamarind water or 2 tamarind
   slices
2 kaffir lime leaves or bay leaves

A common fish in Indonesian kitchens is kakap, *or sea perch. Now, to my delight, I can buy it ready-filleted in Marks and Spencer. Goreng kakap, or fried sea perch, is a favourite dish with my family back home, but I have always preferred curried kakap with green chillies.*

Sprinkle the fish squares with the salt. Put the shallots or onion, garlic, ginger and candlenuts (if used) into a blender with the olive oil and water, and blend until smooth.

In a saucepan heat 3 tbs of the coconut milk. When this is boiling, stir for 1 minute and add the paste from the blender. Continue stirring, add the chillies, galingale powder, coriander, cumin, turmeric, tamarind water or slices and kaffir lime or bay leaves. Then add the rest of the coconut milk. Let this bubble gently for 20–30 minutes, stirring often, until reduced by half.

Carefully put in the fish and continue cooking for 10 minutes. Taste, and adjust seasoning. Serve hot with rice, accompanied by prawn crackers and lots of vegetables or salad.

Saté Ambu-Ambu
Tuna fish saté

Serves 4 as a starter, or 6–8, eaten with other dishes and rice

1½ lb (700 g) fresh tuna fish, minced or cubed
Saté Lilit/Minced Pork Saté Balinese-style marinade (page 30)

I had been trying for years to remember the name of a meaty fish that my grandmother used to cook in Padang Panjang. On my last visit to Indonesia, the same fish appeared on my sister's table. I suggested that it was called ambu-ambu; *she said* tongkol. *When I returned to London, I naturally consulted Alan Davidson's 'Sea Food of South-East Asia', where I found that* tongkol *and* ambu-ambu *are alternative names for mackerel tuna or little tunny.*

I bought some fresh tuna, and decided to saté it, Balinese-style. In fact, other sea fish, like kakap *(sea perch) and* tenggiri *(Spanish mackerel) are also very suitable for this purpose, yet the Balinese themselves generally use fresh-water fish. So you have a wide choice, depending on what is fresh and reasonably-priced at the fishmonger.*

If the fish is cubed, marinate it and put it on sticks as for Saté Bebek/Duck Saté Balinese-style (page 31). If it is minced, mix it with the marinade with your hand, kneading it for a while so that it becomes somewhat sticky. Then put it on sticks as for Saté Lilit.

Grill for 6 minutes, turning several times, or cook in the oven at 180° C/350° F/Gas Mark 4 for about 15 minutes. Serve hot, without sauce or with Nam Chim/Sweet and Sour Chilli Sauce (page 124).

Pangek Bungkus
Sumatran steamed fish with spices and herbs

Serves 10–12, with several other dishes, for a buffet

FOR THE FISH:
1 salmon trout weighing 4–5 lb (about 2 kg), gutted and scaled
2 tbs tamarind water or juice of 1 lime or lemon
1 tsp salt
½ tsp chilli powder
1 stalk lemon grass
2 kaffir lime leaves or bay leaves

FOR THE SPICE MIXTURE
4 shallots
2 cloves garlic
3 candlenuts (optional)
2–4 large red chillies, seeded and chopped
½ pint (300 ml) very thick coconut milk
1 tsp ground coriander
pinch of galingale powder
¼ tsp turmeric powder
salt to taste
2 tbs chopped mint or basil
6 spring onions, thinly sliced

This is best made with fresh-water fish. I make it every time I come back from a visit to my favourite trout farm. You can give each person a whole trout, or for a buffet party cook one or two large salmon trout. In Indonesia, the fish would be wrapped in banana leaves and cooked over charcoal or a wood fire. I cook mine here in the oven wrapped with aluminium foil.

Make 2 diagonal slashes on each side of the fish, then rub the fish inside and out with the tamarind water (or lime or lemon juice), salt and chilli powder. Put the lemon grass and kaffir lime leaves or bay leaves inside the fish. Leave the fish in a cool place while preparing the rest of the ingredients.

Put the shallots, garlic, candlenuts (if used) and chillies in a blender with 4 tbs of the coconut milk, and blend to a smooth paste. Put the paste in a saucepan, bring to the boil, stir and add the ground coriander, galingale powder, turmeric powder and salt. Pour in the rest of the coconut milk and simmer until reduced by half. Adjust the seasoning and leave to cool.

Lay the fish on 3 layers of wide aluminium foil. Pour over it half the thick spiced mixture and a small amount inside the cavity. Turn the fish over and pour the rest of the mixture over the other side. Then spread the chopped mint and spring onion all over the fish. Wrap the aluminium foil around it and steam in the oven at 180° C/350° F/Gas Mark 4 for 35–40 minutes. Serve hot or cold.

Ikan Goreng Dengan Sambal Kemiri

Fried fish with candlenut sauce

Serves 4

FOR THE FISH

4 whole red snapper or red carp,
   cleaned
2 tsp salt
2 tbs tamarind water or lemon juice
a pinch of turmeric powder
vegetable oil for deep frying
2 tbs rice flour or plain flour

FOR THE SAUCE

5 candlenuts
5 shallots, chopped
2 cloves garlic, chopped
3 red chillies, seeded and chopped or 1
   tsp Sambal Ulek/Crushed Red
   Chillies with Salt (page 118)
1 tsp fried shrimp paste (optional)
1 tsp salt
1 tsp sugar
4 fl oz (120 ml) thick coconut milk
2 tbs tamarind water
1 lime, cut into about 10 small pieces

This is usually made with fresh water fish. When my family lived in West Java, a few kilometres outside Cirebon, during the Japanese occupation, we stayed for about a year at my mother's parents' house in a small village called Beran. My grandmother's house was the manor house of that village, a fine modern Dutch-style house, with an idyllic setting. Beyond the big front garden was a small river separating the garden and the main road: a good river for fishing. In the back garden we had, underneath several mango and guava trees, a pond full of ikan emas *or red carp and* mujair, *a little fish that did not grow bigger than the palm of a small adult hand. We had these fish fried quite often, and my mother would make what we all called* sambal muncang *to go with the fried fish and rice. We ate with our hands of course, breaking the crisp fish and dipping it in the sambal. Muncang is the local name for kemiri or candlenuts. Here I use red carp or red snapper, and I don't claim that my sambal kemiri is a copy of my mother's.*

Make 2 deep slashes on both sides of each fish and rub them well, inside and out, with the mixture of salt, tamarind water or lemon juice, and turmeric. Leave in a cool place for at least 30 minutes while preparing the sambal.

Put all the sauce ingredients except the lime pieces into a blender, and blend until smooth. Pour the mixture in a small saucepan, bring to boil and simmer, uncovered, for 12–15 minutes. Taste, adding more sugar or salt if necessary and the pieces of lime. Stir and put into a bowl; serve hot or cold as a dip for the fish.

Heat the oil in a wok or deep fryer to 180° C (350° F). Sprinkle the flour evenly over the fish. Fry 2 fish at a time, turning them over several times, until they are golden brown or the skin is slightly crisp. Serve hot or warm.

Pla Wan
Thai grilled caramelised fish

Serves 4

4 lemon sole or plaice
1 tsp salt
juice of 1 lime
4–6 tbs demerara sugar

I suggest you make this dish in the summer, out of doors on the barbecue. The fish is sprinkled generously with sugar before being grilled. The taste is superb but it can be quite messy if you do this under the grill in the kitchen. I watched this being cooked in a restaurant in Bangkok; when the fish is smoking and quite charred it is served to you piping hot, and you eat it with your fingers. Usually a whole fish is used. Almost any fish can be cooked this way – small whole ones, or fillets or steaks of larger ones.

Rub the fish with the salt and lime juice and leave in a cool place until they are to be grilled. Just before grilling, rub the fish all over with the sugar and grill on charcoal for 3 minutes each side, turning over once. Serve immediately, with a chilli dip (Nam Chim/Sweet and Sour Chilli Sauce, page 124) if you like it hot.

RIGHT: *Homok Talay/Mixed Shellfish in Rich Coconut Milk Sauce – as served at the Blue Elephant, London SW6 (page 41)*

OVERLEAF: *Ikan Kukus Dengan Mangga/Sea Bass in Sweet and Sour Sauce with Mangoes (page 45)*

MEAT, POULTRY AND OFFAL

Meat in tropical countries tends to be leaner and tougher than meat grown in temperate lands where the grass is lusher. This doesn't mean it has less flavour. In fact, it may have more: chickens, certainly, taste more like chickens when they have lived dangerously and ranged freely along the verge of a main road. If you are setting up house in that part of the world, you may find that joints of meat are cut up in ways that are unfamiliar. Even the animals are not quite the same: beef usually comes from buffaloes, and 'lamb' usually means goat. However, none of these considerations is any obstacle to cooking good Thai and Indonesian meat dishes in the west.

Cooking times for some dishes are very short, which is one reason why meat sometimes has to be cut up small; this takes time, but the result will justify it. Some recipes, on the other hand, such as Rendang (see p. 58) demand a very long cooking time, partly perhaps to make tough meat tender but, more importantly, to preserve precious meat for as long as possible. Because meat is expensive, we don't as a rule eat large quantities of it at a sitting, nor do we eat meat by itself; there are always plenty of vegetables and rice with it.

Cooking in bamboo tubes

Gulai Parsanga
Madurese mutton curry

Serves 6–8

1 cup freshly grated coconut or
 desiccated coconut
thin slice of shrimp paste, about 1 in
 (2½ cm) square

FOR THE CURRY MIXTURE
2 tbs vegetable oil
6 shallots or 2 onions, chopped
4 cloves garlic, chopped
1 tsp white pepper
2 tsp ground coriander
1 tsp ground cumin
½ tsp ground nutmeg
¼ tsp galingale powder
1 tsp ground turmeric
2 lb (1 kg) mutton, cut into bite-sized
 pieces

TO FINISH THE CURRY
1 stalk lemon grass or ½ tsp lemon
 grass powder
1 in (2½ cm) cinnamon
6 cloves
1 in (2½ cm) root ginger, chopped
salt to taste
8 fl oz (200 ml) hot water
16 fl oz (450 ml) thick coconut milk

The small island of Madura, off the north-east coast of Java, is famous for its bull-races. Not surprisingly, the Madurese eat a lot of beef. They don't keep sheep, but they do have goats, and this curry ought really to be made with goat's meat; but in countries where goats aren't eaten much, mutton is a good substitute. Like goat, it needs plenty of cooking.

In a wok or frying pan, roast the grated or desiccated coconut, stirring continuously, until golden brown. Then grind finely, either in a grinder or a pestle and mortar. Crush the shrimp paste on a plate with the back of a spoon.

Heat the oil in a saucepan and fry the onion and garlic for 1–2 minutes, then add the other ground ingredients. Stir, and add the meat. Stir again, cover and simmer for 2 minutes. Uncover, and stir in the ground roasted coconut, the lemon grass, cinnamon, cloves, chopped ginger, shrimp paste and salt to taste.

Add the hot water and simmer for 20 minutes. Add the coconut milk and continue to simmer for 20–30 minutes, stirring occasionally, until the sauce is thick and the meat tender. Remove the cinnamon and lemon grass and serve hot, with rice.

Kambing Masak Tauco
Lamb in black bean sauce

Serves 4–6

FOR THE MARINADE
1 tbs light soya sauce
1 tsp mild vinegar

*1½ lb (700 g) lean meat from a leg of
    lamb, thinly sliced*
4 tbs black tauco
4 fl oz (120 ml) peanut oil
5 shallots, thinly sliced
4 cloves garlic, chopped
½ in (1 cm) root ginger, chopped
*1 tbs dark soya sauce, preferably
    Indonesian kecap manis*
*4 green chillies, seeded and sliced
    diagonally*

Most Indonesians prefer yellow bean sauce to black. Both have the same name, 'tauco'; yellow tauco is used mostly with chicken or vegetables, when you want plenty of sauce; for a 'dry-fried' dish black tauco is better, as the Chinese know. In a Chinese restaurant you would expect this dish to be made with pork. People of my parents' generation, if they were strict Moslems, would not eat in Chinese restaurants, but younger people do, simply asking that there should be no pork in the cooking. So nowadays the cook will quite happily make a dish of lamb in black bean sauce for you, and it will be very good – the combination of black beans with green chillies is just right. Note that the meat can be marinated well in advance if desired.

Rub the sliced meat with the light soya sauce and malt vinegar well. Put in a bowl and leave to marinate for 1 hour or more.

Soak the black tauco in cold water for 10 minutes, then drain and rinse. Mash the tauco, not too smoothly, on a plate with the back of a spoon.

Heat the oil in a wok or frying pan, and fry the meat in batches for 3 minutes each time. Take out with a slotted spoon and drain on absorbent paper. Retain about 2 tbs of the oil and discard the rest. Fry the shallots, garlic and ginger, stirring continuously for 2 minutes. Add the green chillies, the mashed black tauco, and dark soya sauce; continue stir-frying for 1 minute, then add the meat. Stir continuously again for 2 minutes. Serve hot with plain boiled rice.

Kambing Asam Pedas
Hot and sour lamb

Serves 4–6

FOR THE MEAT

1½ lb (700 g) lean meat from a leg of
 lamb
1 tsp salt

4 shallots
2 cloves garlic
½ in (1 cm) root ginger
2 large red chillies, seeded, or ½ tsp
 chilli powder
4 candlenuts or 4 fl oz (120 ml) thick
 coconut milk
1 tsp ground coriander
6 oz (175 g) can of bamboo shoots
1 green or yellow pepper, seeded
4 fl oz (120 ml) vegetable oil
3 tbs tamarind water or 2 tamarind
 slices or 2 tbs mild vinegar
4 fl oz (120 ml) cold water
salt to taste

*Most Indonesian dishes with hot and sour sauce come from West
Sumatra, where I was born. My grandmother would always cook
this with tamarind and lots of red chillies crushed into a smooth
paste. The sauce was very red, really hot and sour, and delicious.*

*The recipe that follows will look and taste just as good but will not
be burning hot. If tamarind is not available, it is quite all right to use
mild vinegar.*

Cut the meat into thin slices, then cut diagonally into small
bite-sized pieces. Put in a bowl, and rub well with the salt. Set
aside in a cool place for 10 minutes or so.

Put the shallots, garlic, ginger, red chillies, candlenuts or
coconut milk into a blender and blend until smooth. If you are
using candlenuts, add 4 tbs water to the mixture. Add the
ground coriander.

Cut the bamboo shoots and the pepper into diamond-shaped
slices. Blanch the pepper.

In a wok or large saucepan, heat the oil and fry the meat in
batches for 3 minutes each time. Take out with a slotted spoon
and put on absorbent paper to drain. Discard the remaining
oil, except for about 2 tablespoonfuls. Fry the shallot paste,
stirring continuously, for 3 minutes. Add the tamarind water or
tamarind slices or vinegar, the bamboo shoots and the water,
and simmer for 3 minutes. Add the meat and continue stirring
for 2 minutes. Then add the pepper and stir for 1 minute
longer. Taste, and add salt if necessary. If using tamarind
slices, discard these before serving. Serve hot with rice or
pasta.

Musaman Curry
Beef curry with peanuts

Serves 4–6

FOR BLENDING THE CURRY PASTE

5 shallots
2 cloves garlic
1 in (2½ cm) stalk lemon grass, outer leaves discarded
2 tbs chopped coriander root and stalk
4 red chillies, seeded
1 tbs coriander seed
1 tsp cumin seed
2 cardamom seeds
2 tbs oil
2 tbs water

TO FINISH THE CURRY PASTE

½ tsp galingale powder
½ tsp ground nutmeg
½ tsp ground cinnamon
2–3 cloves
1 tbs crumbled shrimp paste

2 tbs vegetable oil
1½ lb (700 g) brisket or good stewing steak, cut into 1 in (2½ cm) cubes
3 tbs tamarind water or 2 tamarind slices
1 tbs palm sugar or demerara sugar
2 kaffir lime leaves
1½ pints (900 ml) thick coconut milk
salt
1 small pineapple, cut into small cubes (optional)
4 oz (120 g) roasted peanuts, roughly crushed

The sauce of this curry needs to be dark brown and very thick, and as well as roasted peanuts it is quite customary to add small cubes of fresh ripe pineapple a minute or two before cooking is finished.

Put all the ingredients that are to be blended in the paste on a baking tray and roast in the oven at 180° C/350° F/Gas Mark 4 for 10 minutes. Alternatively, put them in a heavy skillet or frying pan and brown on the stove, shaking the pan frequently. Transfer to a blender, add the oil and water, and blend until smooth. Add the galingale powder, ground nutmeg, ground cinnamon, cloves and shrimp paste.

In a large saucepan, heat the 2 tbs oil and fry the curry paste, stirring continuously with a wooden spoon, for 3 minutes. Add the meat, stir until all the pieces are coated with the paste, then add the tamarind water or tamarind slices. Cover and simmer for 3 minutes. Uncover, and add the sugar, kaffir lime leaves and coconut milk.

Bring gently to the boil, then simmer for about 1½ hours until the sauce becomes very thick. Stir frequently when the sauce starts to thicken. Taste and add salt if necessary. Add the pineapple cubes, if used, and the peanuts. Stir for 1 more minute and serve hot, with plain boiled rice.

Gaeng Ped Neua
Red curry of beef

Serves 4–6

2½ lb (1 kg) brisket or braising steak
5 shallots or 1 onion
3 cloves garlic
½ tsp galingale
3 coriander roots, chopped
5 strips of dried kaffir lime peel
1 tbs roasted coriander seed
1 tsp roasted cumin seed
½ tsp ground nutmeg
½ tsp ground mace
15 large dried red chillies, seeded or 1
    tsp chilli powder plus 2 tsp paprika
1 stalk fresh lemon grass, chopped
2 tsp crumbled shrimp paste
1 tsp ground white pepper
1 tbs salt
2½ pints (1.4 l) coconut milk

This Thai curry somewhat resembles the traditional Rendang from West Sumatra (page 58), but the taste is different as this curry has many more spices in it.

Trim and discard most of the fat from the beef, then cut into ¾ inch (2 cm) cubes.

Put the remaining ingredients, with 5 tbs of the coconut milk, into a blender and blend to a smooth paste.

In a large saucepan, heat about 4 fl oz (130 ml) of the coconut milk. When it boils, add the paste, stir and simmer until the coconut milk becomes oil. Continue stirring for another 2 minutes, then add the meat and stir again until all the meat has been coated by the paste. Add the rest of the coconut milk. Bring back to the boil, lower the heat and let the curry bubble gently for about 2 hours until the meat is tender and the sauce thick. Taste, add salt if necessary, and serve hot with boiled rice.

This curry can be reheated in a saucepan or in a microwave oven. It can also be frozen successfully. Thaw out completely before reheating.

Nua Pud Prik

Beef fried with green peppers

Serves 4

1 lb (450 g) rump steak, topside of beef or leftover roast beef

FOR THE MARINADE
2 tsp cornflour or potato flour
1 tbs light soya sauce
1/4 tsp chilli powder
1 in (2 1/2 cm) root ginger, finely chopped

1–2 medium-sized green peppers, seeded
8 oz (225 g) baby corn (optional)
about 4 fl oz (130 ml) peanut or sunflower oil
4 spring onions, cut diagonally into strips
2 cloves garlic, crushed
1/4 tsp chilli powder
2 tbs light soya sauce
1 tbs fish sauce
1 tsp sugar
1 tsp rice vinegar or white malt vinegar

This is a standard dish in Thai, Chinese or Malaysian restaurants. The ingredients vary from one area to another. I often use leftovers from the Sunday roast beef. With roast beef, the marinade and initial frying are not necessary.

Trim the meat and cut across the grain into bite-sized pieces. Mix the marinade well in a bowl, add the slices of beef and mix again so that every slice is well coated. Leave in a cool place for at least 30 minutes.

Cut the green pepper into strips about 3/4 in (2 cm) wide, then cut each strip diagonally into 4 or 5 pieces. Cut each baby corn diagonally also, to about the same size as the peppers.

In a wok or frying pan, heat the oil. Fry the green pepper in batches for 2 minutes each time. Take out with a slotted spoon and drain on absorbent paper. Do the same with the baby corn (if used). Strain the oil into a bowl to get rid of any fragments of baby corn.

Pour the strained oil back into the wok or frying pan, heat, and fry the beef, in batches, stirring continuously, for 2 minutes each time. Remove with a slotted spoon to drain. By the time you finish frying the beef, there will be just enough oil left to go on to the next step. If there seems to be still too much, discard some, leaving about 2 tbs only.

Heat the remaining oil, add the spring onions, garlic and chilli powder, stir, and add the soya sauce, fish sauce and sugar. Stir again, and add the beef, green peppers and baby corn. Continue stirring and turning for a minute or so. Taste, add salt if necessary, and serve immediately with rice or noodles.

Rendang

A traditional West Sumatran dish

Serves 10–12

3 lb (1½ kg) brisket, silverside, or
  good stewing steak
6 shallots, thinly sliced
4 cloves garlic
1 in (2½ cm) root ginger, roughly
  chopped
6 red chillies, seeded and roughly
  chopped, or 3 tsp chilli powder
3 pints (1.8 l) coconut milk
1 tsp turmeric
½ tsp galingale
1 salam leaf or bayleaf
1 stalk fresh lemon grass, bruised
2 tsp salt

Rendang is nothing like a curry. A well-cooked one is brown, sometimes almost black. It should be chunky and dry, yet succulent, with the dryness of meat that has absorbed its juices and its sauce during a long period of cooking. The cooking process is, I think, unique, for it is the only dish that I know of that passes from boiling to frying without any interruption. The cooking time is therefore very long.

There are several quite different basic ingredients you can use as the foundation of the dish. For instance there is a 'Rendang Nangka' (Jackfruit Rendang), a lovely vegetarian dish. The traditional Rendang, as I learnt it from my grandmother in Padang Panjang, West Sumatra, used buffalo meat, and it was almost always cooked in large quantities.

Cut the meat into biggish cubes. Put the shallots, garlic, ginger and chillies in a blender or a food processor, and reduce to a purée. Put all these ingredients and the coconut milk in a large wok or saucepan with the turmeric and galingale. Add the salam leaf, lemon grass, salt and meat, which must be completely covered by the coconut milk. Stir, and start cooking on a medium heat, uncovered. Let this bubble for 1½ hours, stirring from time to time. By this time the coconut milk will be quite thick.

Transfer the whole dish into a wok if a saucepan was used to start with. Again let this bubble for ½ hour, stirring occasionally. You'll notice by now the coconut milk already starting to become oily. The dish now needs to be stirred frequently. Taste and add more salt if necessary.

When it becomes thick and brown, stir all the time for about 15 minutes, until the oil has almost disappeared, absorbed by the meat. Now the dish is ready. Serve hot with plenty of rice.

Note: Rendang will keep for more than 1 week in the fridge, and can be reheated as often as you like. It can be frozen successfully, and kept frozen for 5–6 months. Thaw completely before you heat it in an ovenproof dish in a moderate oven for 10–15 minutes.

Gulai Daging Dengan Kentang
Beef stew with potatoes

Serves 6–8

FOR THE MEAT

*2 lb (1 kg) brisket or good stewing
  steak, cut into ½ in (1 cm) cubes*
1 tbs rice flour or plain flour
1 tsp salt
1 tbs tamarind water or 1 tsp vinegar

*2 lb (1 kg) small new potatoes, scraped
  or large potatoes, cubed*
4 fl oz (120 ml) vegetable oil
6 shallots or 2 onions, finely chopped
4 cloves garlic, finely chopped
2 tsp ground coriander
½ tsp chilli powder
½ tsp turmeric powder
½ tsp ginger powder
2 kaffir lime leaves or bay leaves
1½ pints (900 ml) thick coconut milk
salt
*2 lb (1 kg) spaghetti marrow or
  pumpkin, peeled and cubed*

In Indonesia we used to make this in the time of the Japanese occupation, when food, especially meat, was scarce and very expensive. Any vegetables that we could dig or pick from the garden went into the stew, not just potatoes. But when good ingredients are available this will make an excellent but still economical dish for a large party or a family gathering, adding to the potato one other vegetable. Here I suggest spaghetti marrow or pumpkin. Serve the stew with garlic bread, pasta or rice and salad, or just a salad.

Put the meat in a bowl and rub the pieces well with flour, salt, and tamarind water or vinegar. Keep aside while preparing the rest of the ingredients. Keep the prepared potatoes in a bowl of salted water.

In a large saucepan, heat the oil and fry the meat in 3 or 4 batches for 3 minutes each time, stirring continuously. Remove with a slotted spoon to drain.

Keep about 2 tbs of the oil, and discard the rest. Fry the chopped shallots or onions and chopped garlic, stirring continuously, for 2 minutes. Add the ground and powdered ingredients, stir, and add kaffir lime leaves or bay leaves, half the coconut milk, and salt to taste. Stir, bring to the boil, and add the meat. Simmer gently for 40 minutes. By the end of this time the meat should be almost tender and the sauce should be getting thick.

Add the rest of the coconut milk, continue cooking for 10 minutes. Add the potato, cook for another 10 minutes, then add the marrow or pumpkin and cook for 10 minutes more or until the potatoes and marrow or pumpkin are cooked. The sauce should not be too thick. Serve hot.

This gulai can be reheated and will mix well with any kind of hot or cold buffet party food.

Saté Daging
Beef saté

Serves 4

FOR THE MARINADE
3 shallots, thinly sliced
2 cloves garlic, chopped (optional)
1 tbs white malt vinegar
2 tsp ground coriander
½–1 tsp chilli powder
½ tsp salt
2 tbs light soya sauce
2 tbs peanut or olive oil

1 lb (450 g) rump steak, cut into ¾ in (2 cm) cubes
8–12 × 10 in (25 cm) wooden saté sticks or metal skewers

This is, I suppose, the classic Indonesian dish that everyone knows. It came originally from the Middle East and is closely related to shish kebab, with which it obviously has a lot in common. As long as you use a tender meat (rump steak is my favourite) you can hardly go wrong.

Mix all the ingredients for the marinade in a bowl, add the meat and stir well to make sure every piece is well covered. Leave for at least 2 hours or overnight in the fridge.

Discard the marinade and divide the meat between the skewers. Grill, turning several times, for 6–8 minutes. Grilling on charcoal will give an even better flavour.

Eat hot, with saté sauce or sambal kecap. In Indonesia, we usually also sprinkle fried shallots or crisp fried onions over the saté just before serving.

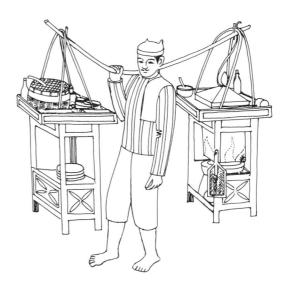

Dendeng Daging
Dry-fried (or grilled) beef

Serves 4–6

FOR THE MARINADE
8 cloves garlic
2 shallots
1 tsp black peppercorns
1 tbs coriander seeds
*2 candlenuts or 5 tbs thick coconut
   cream*
2 tbs tamarind water or 2 tsp vinegar
½ tsp ground nutmeg
½ in (1 cm) cinnamon stick
1 tsp salt
1 tbs dark soya sauce or kecap manis
2 tbs sunflower oil or olive oil

*1½ lb (700 g) rump steak, thinly
   sliced*
*2 tbs grated palm sugar or soft brown
   sugar (optional)*

As with saté, the flavour of Dendeng depends very much on the marinade. Of course it also depends on the meat; you need a tender cut, as the cooking time is very short.

The traditional Dendeng Daging is sweet. After being marinated the beef is dried in the tropical sun and then deep-fried until crisp. It should be tender and brittle, but if the drying is not just right it can become leathery and tough. In this recipe, however, you will not need to worry about whether the day is sunny or not, because there is no need to dry the meat. I like a good garlicky marinade, but use less garlic if you prefer.

Put all the ingredients for the marinade in a blender and blend until smooth. In a bowl put the slices of beef with the paste, mixing them thoroughly so that every slice of beef is well coated. Marinade for at least 2 hours, or overnight. If you like your dendeng rather sweet, coat the slices with the sugar before cooking.

Grill or shallow-fry the meat in a non-stick frying pan for not more than 3 minutes in all, turning the slices over once. Serve immediately. My choice with dendeng is fried rice (page 80), with a salad or green vegetables.

Moo Wan

Sweet pork with marigold

Serves 4

FOR THE PORK
1 lb (450 g) fillet of pork
1 tbs dark soya sauce
1/4 tsp salt

FOR THE SAUCE
2 tbs peanut oil
1 onion, finely chopped
2 tbs grated palm sugar or demerara
   sugar
1/2 tsp ground white pepper
2 tbs fish sauce
1 tbs dark soya sauce
1/4 tsp salt
1/4 tsp pepper
8 tbs hot water
1 tsp fried shrimp paste
2 tbs chopped coriander leaves
a handful of marigold petals

My Thai friend Noot (Mrs Kamolvan Punyashthiti) has given me a number of recipes for this book. Some I have adapted a little, but this one I keep exactly, I hope, as she would cook it herself. She told me that it looks particularly good if you sprinkle it with marigold petals, and that French marigolds are best. Use other flower petals instead, if you like – nasturtiums are quite nice – or leave the petals out altogether. But mix some shrimp paste with the pork at the end of cooking. Serve the sweet pork on top of plain boiled fragrant Thai rice.

Slice the pork thinly into small bite-sized pieces, leaving some of the fat on. Rub the pieces well with the soya sauce and salt. Keep in a cool place while you prepare the rest of the ingredients.

Heat the oil in a wok or frying pan, and fry the onion until soft. Add the sugar and fish sauce, and stir vigorously with a wooden spoon until the sugar has caramelised.

Add the pork, stir-fry for 3 minutes, then add the soya sauce, salt, pepper and hot water, and continue cooking on quite a high heat for 3 minutes, stirring frequently. Add the shrimp paste, and stir-fry again for a few seconds. Serve hot with rice, sprinkled with chopped coriander leaves and marigold petals.

Babi Asam Pedas
Hot and sour pork

Serves 4

There are different versions of this dish all over South-East Asia. Mine is one that I used during the three years when I had an oriental delicatessen in Wimbledon; I know it works well, and my customers liked it.

FOR THE PORK
1 tsp salt
2 tsp white malt vinegar
1 lb (450 g) lean fillet of pork, cut into ³⁄4 in (2 cm) cubes

FOR THE SAUCE
4 shallots or 1 onion
2 cloves garlic
1 in (2¹⁄2 cm) root ginger
3 candlenuts (optional)
2 large red chillies, seeded and chopped, or 1¹⁄2 tsp chilli powder
4 fl oz (120 ml) sunflower or olive oil
6 tbs water
3 tbs white malt vinegar
1 tbs sugar
6 oz (175 g) can bamboo shoots, drained and rinsed
salt to taste
3 tbs chopped mint or basil

Rub the salt and vinegar into the pork and leave for 30 minutes.

Put the shallots, garlic, ginger, candlenuts and red chillies into a blender, add 2 tbs of the oil and 2 tbs of the water and blend into a smooth paste.

Heat the oil in a wok or frying pan and fry the pieces of pork in batches for 4–5 minutes each time. Remove with a slotted spoon to drain.

Discard the oil, except for about 2 tbs. Heat this and fry the paste from the blender, stirring continuously for 3 minutes. Add the vinegar and sugar, stir and add the remaining water, the bamboo shoots and the pork. Simmer for 2 minutes; taste, and add salt if necessary. Stir again for another minute, add the chopped mint or basil, stir, and serve immediately with rice or boiled new potatoes.

This dish can be frozen satisfactorily. Thaw completely before reheating in a saucepan, stirring occasionally until hot.

Prik Yuak Sod Sai
Stuffed chillies in nets

Serves 6–8

12–16 large mild green chillies

FOR THE STUFFING
8 oz (225 g) minced pork
4 oz (120 g) uncooked prawns or
*   shrimps, peeled and minced*
2 tbs chopped coriander leaves
2 cloves garlic, chopped
2 tbs chopped spring onions
6 water chestnuts, chopped roughly
1 tbs light soya sauce
1 tbs fish sauce
1 tsp salt
1 tsp sugar
1 egg

FOR THE NETS
4 eggs
a large pinch of salt
1 tbs olive oil

For this, choose the largest green chillies you can find. They should be light green or yellowish in colour, not dark – the dark ones are much hotter.

Cut the tops off the chillies and scoop out the seeds.

Mix the minced pork and prawns thoroughly with a fork. Add the chopped coriander leaves, garlic, spring onions and water chestnuts and continue mixing, either with the fork or by hand. Add the soya sauce and fish sauce, and season with salt and sugar. Finally add the egg and mix everything thoroughly. Divide this stuffing into 12 or 16 portions and stuff the chillies with it, then steam them for 12–15 minutes.

Now make the nets from the 4 eggs. Break them into a bowl and add the salt. Flick the fingers of one hand lightly through the eggs once or twice; this is to break up the yolks and distribute the salt, without totally mixing yolks and whites.

Rub a non-stick frying pan with oil and heat it until it is just warm. Dip the fingers of one hand into the egg and move your hand from side to side, forward and back above the frying pan, letting the liquid egg run from your finger-tips to form a network of lines. Leave the egg-net for about a minute, then lift it carefully onto a flat plate.

Continue making nets until all the egg is used up. Roll and wrap the stuffed chillies in the nets. Serve warm or cold as a snack with drinks or as an accompaniment to a rice meal.

Muh Pud Prik

Slices of pork fried with ginger and mushrooms

Serves 4

FOR THE MARINADE
1 tbs light soya sauce
1 tbs cornflour or plain flour
a pinch of chilli powder
1 tbs rice vinegar

1 lb (450 g) fillet of pork, thinly sliced
5 tbs oil
8 oz (225 g) button mushrooms,
  halved
2 cloves garlic, crushed
1 in (2½ cm) root ginger, chopped
4 fl oz (120 ml) hot water
1 tbs dark soya sauce
1 tbs fish sauce
salt and pepper to taste

FOR THE GARNISH
1 tbs chopped coriander leaf
2 tbs chopped spring onions

If you have had this dish in a restaurant you will probably have noticed that the sauce was thickened with cornflour immediately before serving. This produces a gooey sauce which I find unappetising. If you follow my method, using the flour to marinate the meat, the sauce will appear thickened but not sticky, and it will taste much better.

Mix together the marinade ingredients, add the pork slices and marinate for at least 2 hours.

Heat the oil in a wok or frying pan. Fry the mushrooms for 2 minutes. Remove with a slotted spoon and spread on absorbent paper. Heat the oil again, add half of the pork and stir fry for 2 minutes. Remove the pork with a slotted spoon into a bowl. Fry the remaining pork for 2 minutes, then remove to the bowl.

By now you should have some clear oil in the wok or frying pan, with some flour from the marinade sticking to the bottom. This will thicken the sauce at the end of cooking. Discard most of the oil, leaving about 1 tablespoonful.

Heat this oil, then add the crushed garlic and ginger. Stir, and add the water, soya sauce and fish sauce. Continue stirring. The sauce should by now be starting to thicken. Add the pork and mushrooms and season to taste. Stir-fry for 2 minutes.

Just before serving, add the garnish. Stir for ½ minute more and serve immediately, with plain boiled rice or noodles or pasta.

Tod Man Muh
Spicy minced pork fried in batter

Serves 4–6

FOR THE BATTER
2 oz (60 g) rice flour or plain flour
1/2 tsp salt
1/2 tsp ground white pepper
4 fl oz (120 ml) cold water
2 tsp olive oil

1 1/2 lb (700 g) minced pork
5 shallots, chopped
4 cloves garlic, chopped
4 red chillies, seeded and chopped
2 coriander roots, chopped
2 tbs chopped coriander leaves
4 fresh kaffir lime leaves, shredded, or
    dried kaffir lime leaves, crushed
2 oz (60 g) yard-long beans or French
    beans, sliced into thin rounds
2 tsp sugar
1/2 tsp salt
2 tsp light soya sauce
1 tbs fish sauce
2 tbs olive oil
vegetable oil for deep frying

Some people spell this Tod Mun. There are several dishes with this name; this one is made with minced pork. Every country has its own meatball dish, made of different kinds of meat. This Thai version is good and spicy. The meatballs or cakes are normally flattened a little, like Tod Man Pla Krai/Savoury Fish Cake (page 106), before being deep fried.

Mix all the ingredients for the batter in a bowl, stirring vigorously with a wooden spoon; this batter should be quite thin. Then in a separate bowl mix well the minced pork with all the other ingredients, including the olive oil. Leave to marinate for 30–40 minutes, or overnight in the fridge.

Take about 1 tbs of the meat, put it on the palm of your hand and form it into a ball. Make all the meat into meat balls in the same way. Everything up to this point can be done in advance and the meat balls are then stored in the fridge or freezer for use later. Thaw out completely before frying.

To cook, flatten the meat balls between the palms of your hands, pressing them gently. Then dip one by one in the batter and deep-fry 5 or 6 at a time for 3–4 minutes in a wok or deep fryer. Remove with a slotted spoon and drain on kitchen paper. Serve hot with rice and a vegetable dish. The Tomato Sauce on page 123 is good to serve with this. Reheat it, and garnish with Goreng Bawang/Fried Shallots (page 120).

Gaeng Keo Wan Kai
Green curry of chicken

Serves 4–6

1 chicken, weighing about 2½–3 lb (1–1½ kg), or 2 lb (1 kg) chicken breast and thigh meat

FOR THE PASTE
4 shallots, chopped
3 cloves garlic, chopped
½ stalk lemon grass, outer leaves removed
1 tbs chopped coriander root
¾ in (2 cm) piece fresh galingale, chopped
1 tsp grated kaffir lime peel
1 tsp ground pepper
1 tbs roasted coriander seed
1 tsp roasted cumin seed
½ tsp each ground mace and nutmeg
5 fresh green chillies, seeded
1 green pepper (optional)
2 tbs chopped coriander leaves
½ tsp shrimp paste
2 tsp salt

2 tbs vegetable oil
2 pints (1.2 l) coconut milk, made from 8 oz (225 g) desiccated coconut or 1⅓ pints (850 ml) chicken stock and ½ pint (300 ml) unsweetened yogurt
1 lb (450 g) pea aubergines or small new potatoes

The sauce for this Thai curry can be very liquid and runny, or it can be reduced and made quite thick. I myself like it not too thick, especially if I can find pea aubergines to put in it rather than new potatoes. The sauce is made from curry paste mixed with coconut milk; if you do not like coconut milk, substitute plain unsweetened yogurt or, better still, the creamy Greek yogurt.

Bone the chicken and cut the meat into ¾ in (2 cm) cubes. If you are going to make the curry sauce with stock and yogurt, use the chicken bones to make the stock.

Blend all the ingredients for the paste together in a food processor, or crush and grind them together. Heat the oil in a saucepan and fry the paste in it, stirring all the time, for 2–3 minutes. Then add the chicken pieces and stir until all the pieces are well coated with the paste. Turn down the heat, cover the pan and let it simmer for 4 minutes.

If using coconut milk, stir in and simmer, stirring frequently, for 50 minutes. Add the pea-aubergines or new potatoes, and continue cooking for 10–15 minutes or until the aubergines (or potatoes) are cooked. Serve hot with plain boiled rice.

If using stock and yogurt, add the stock instead of the coconut milk. Simmer for 50 minutes, then remove the pan from the heat for 10 minutes. Stir in the yogurt, bring the mixture slowly back to a gentle boil (to prevent curdling). Add the pea-aubergines or potatoes, and stir frequently until cooked (as above).

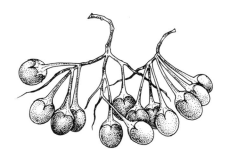

Peek Kai Yod Sai
Stuffed chicken wings

Serves 4–6

12 chicken wings
4 oz (120 g) minced pork
4 oz (120 g) uncooked peeled shrimps,
    minced
4 spring onions, thinly sliced
roots and stalks of 2 coriander plants,
    chopped
1 red or green chilli, seeded and chop-
    ped, or ¼ tsp chilli powder
2 cloves garlic, chopped
1 tbs light soya sauce
1 tsp sugar
1 tsp salt
1 egg
3 tbs rice flour or fine fresh
    breadcrumbs
oil for deep frying

This is a dish you will find equally often in Thailand and in Indonesia, and indeed in several other South-East Asian countries. Maybe it was a Chinese dish originally; I remember eating it often in my local Chinese restaurant when I lived in Yogyakarta. The Chinese and the Thais use pork as one of the ingredients for the stuffing, and what follows is the Thai version of the recipe. By omitting the pork and the coriander root, you will make it an Indonesian dish.

Using a sharp knife, slit the skin of each chicken wing from the wing-tip joint along the length of the wing. Carefully separate the bones at the joints, then remove the bones and the meat from the skin. If you can leave the bony wing-tip in place, attached to the skin, so much the better; it makes a good handle if you eat with your fingers. However, this is not really important.

To make the stuffing, mince the chicken meat and mix it with the remaining ingredients (except the egg and rice flour or breadcrumbs). Beat the egg and spread the flour or bread-crumbs on a flat plate.

Divide the stuffing into 12 portions and roll each portion in the skin of a chicken wing. When all 12 are done, dip them one at a time in the beaten egg and roll them over in the rice flour or breadcrumbs.

Steam the stuffed wings for 4 minutes. Leave to cool before deep-frying them, a few at a time, until golden brown. Serve whole as snacks, or slice them like sausages and serve with salad. These slices are also good for mixing with stir-fried vegetables or fried noodles.

These stuffed wings can be frozen after steaming, and then fried straight from the freezer.

Ayam Rica-Rica
Grilled chicken, Menado style

Serves 4

FOR THE CHICKEN
*2 small chickens, weighing about
    2½ lb (1¼ kg) each
1 tsp salt
juice of 1 lime
2 tbs oil or melted butter*

FOR THE SPICE PASTE
*10 shallots or 2 onions
4 cloves garlic
4 red chillies, seeded
2 in (5 cm) root ginger
½ in (1 cm) slice of shrimp paste
    (optional)
2 tbs oil
2 tbs water
4 tomatoes, peeled, seeded and chopped
    (optional)
½ tbs salt*

Rica-rica (pronounced reetja-reetja) is usually very hot. A friend of mine who gave me this recipe said she used up to 20 large red chillies for one chicken. The idea is that the whole chicken should be covered in the red chilli paste. To make the same quantity of paste with fewer chillies, I use more shallots and, like the Menadonese, I also put in some tomatoes; but as there are many areas of Indonesia where tomatoes aren't used, I have shown these as optional. I wrap the chicken in aluminium foil to preserve the sauce in the early stages of cooking.

Split the chickens lengthwise into halves and trim off some of the skin, fat and bones. Rub the four halves with salt, lime juice and oil or butter. Leave in a cool place while you prepare the other ingredients.

Put the shallots or onions, garlic, chillies, ginger and shrimp paste (if used) into a blender with the oil and water. Blend until smooth. Pour this paste into a saucepan, bring to the boil and stir continuously for 4 minutes. Add the chopped tomatoes and continue cooking, and stirring, for 1 minute. Taste, and add salt if necessary. Remove from the stove and leave to cool.

When the paste is cool, use half of it to rub over the chickens, rubbing under the skin as well. Then put each half chicken on aluminium foil. Put the remaining paste on top of each half-chicken. Wrap the halves in the foil, making the join on the top of each parcel.

Cook in the oven at 170° C/325° F/Gas Mark 3 for 45 minutes. Then open up the foil wrapping and grill for 4–6 minutes. Slide the chickens and the sauce onto a serving dish and serve at once.

Ayam Betutu
Balinese chicken

Serves 4

4 chicken breasts or 8 chicken thighs,
   boned but not skinned
4 oz (120 g) curly kale or vine leaves
   or young courgette leaves, blanched
   and shredded

FOR THE SPICE MIXTURE
5 shallots
4 cloves garlic
5 red chillies, seeded, or 1 tsp chilli
   powder
2 candlenuts or 5 tbs very thick
   coconut milk
3 tsp coriander seed
2 tsp cumin seed
2 cloves
1 cinnamon stick, about 2 in (5 cm)
1/2 tsp ground nutmeg
1/2 tsp ground turmeric
1/2 tsp galingale powder
1/2 tsp white pepper
2 in (5 cm) piece of lemon grass or 1/2
   tsp lemon grass powder
2 in (5 cm) shrimp paste
juice of 1 lime
2 tbs vegetable oil
2 tbs water

2 tbs oil
2 tbs salt

This, made with duck, is a traditional Balinese dish; the monks of Ubud still cook it in the old-fashioned way, leaving it for six or seven hours in the embers of a fire laid in a shallow trench. The duck is stuffed and wrapped in seludang mayang, *the flower-sheath of a particular kind of palm, then layers and layers of banana leaves. An excellent alternative is to use aluminium foil, as described here; but remember that you need plenty – the chicken must be wrapped in several layers. I watched a Balinese friend cook a young chicken, using the same recipe but in an electric oven; it tasted extremely good. This is really her recipe, except that instead of the whole chicken I suggest using just the thighs and breast, boned but with the skin still on.*

The leaves for the stuffing should be young cassava leaves, which I have not been able to find in Britain. Instead, I use curly kale in autumn and winter; in spring and summer, I use very young vine or courgette leaves; alternatively spinach, which is available any time. Whatever leaves you use, you need to blanch them first, squeeze out excess water and shred them finely.

Don't be put off by the long list of spices. The result is well worth the trouble of getting them all together.

Process all the ingredients for the spice mixture in a food processor. (Or use a pestle and mortar if you prefer.) Fry this paste in the oil, stirring continuously, for about 5 minutes or until the smell of raw shallots and garlic has been replaced by a pleasant spicy fragrance. Add half the salt, and leave to cool.

Mix half of the cooled paste in a bowl with the shredded leaves. Then rub the remaining salt evenly into the chicken pieces. Rub the spices into every part of the chicken, including under the skin. Stuff the shredded leaves under the skin, spreading them evenly.

Lay a chicken breast or two thighs on a piece of aluminium foil and wrap loosely. When all the pieces are wrapped, you will have four packets. Line a baking tray with three layers of aluminium foil. Lay the four packets on the tray in pairs, one packet on top of another. Fold the foil lining of the baking tray over the top to make one parcel. Everything up to this point can

Serves 4

1 chicken, weighing about 2¹/₂–3
(1–1¹/₂ kg), cut into serving p

FOR THE MARINADE
3 tbs tamarind water
a pinch of ground turmeric
1 tsp salt
¹/₂ tsp ground coriander
¹/₂ tsp ground white pepper

oil for deep frying

FOR THE CHILLI COATING
8–10 large red chillies, seeded
chopped or roughly chopped
6 shallots or 2 onions, thinly s
2 tbs vegetable oil
¹/₂ tsp salt

be done the day before, and the parcel can be left in the fridge overnight so that the chicken marinates thoroughly.

Cook in the oven at 150° C/325° F/Gas Mark 2 for 2–3 hours. Turn down the oven to 110° C/225° F/Gas Mark ¹/₄ after the first hour. To serve, unwrap the parcel and packets and put the chicken pieces straight onto the dinner plates, or put onto a warm serving dish together with the cooking juices.

Serve with rice or noodles or boiled new potatoes and vegetables.

Ayam Betutu can also be eaten cold, sliced thin, with a salad. You can of course cook duck breasts in the same way, but remember to pour off the surplus oil when you open up the 'packets'.

Serves 4–6

1 whole chicken, weighing abo
   3–3½ lb (1½–1¾ kg), wi
   lets; or 2¼ lb (1 kg) chickei
   (from breast and thighs) pli
   chicken livers
2 tbs lemon or lime juice
½ tsp salt

FOR THE AROMATIC MIX7
4 shallots, thinly sliced
2 large green chillies, seeded (
   chopped
1 in (2½ cm) root ginger, fir
   chopped
3 cloves garlic, finely chopped
½ stalk lemon grass, outer l(
   discarded, finely chopped
1 pandanus leaf, finely chop,
4 kaffir lime leaves, finely cl
4 spring onions, thinly slice(
2 tbs chopped mint
2 tbs chopped basil
2 green tomatoes, finely cho,
2 tbs olive oil

Serves 4–6

12 oz (350 g) long-grain rice
12 fl oz (350 ml) coconut
   milk
1 tsp salt
1 salam leaf or bay leaf
2 tbs vegetable oil or clarified butter

Serves 4–6

12 oz (350 g) long-grain rice
2 tbs vegetable oil
1 tsp turmeric
1 tsp ground coriander
½ tsp cumin
12 fl oz (350 ml) stock or
   coconut milk
1 stick cinnamon
1 clove
½ tsp salt
1 salam leaf or bay leaf

RIGHT: *Kambing Asam Pedas/Hot and Sour Lamb (page 54) and Sen Mee Pud/Rice-Stick Noodles with Pork and Beansprouts (page 88)*

Nasi Lemak
Coconut rice

Boiling the rice in coconut milk gives it an extra flavour that everyone seems to like. Use either full coconut milk or the thinner liquid that is left after the cream has been removed for use in another dish.

Soak the rice in cold water for 1 hour, wash and drain. Heat the oil or butter in a saucepan and sauté the rice for 3 minutes.

Add the coconut milk, salt and salam leaf or bay leaf, and simmer for about 10 minutes until the rice has absorbed all the liquid. Lower the heat, cover as tightly as possible and leave to cook for 10–12 minutes. Alternatively, put the half-cooked rice into a rice steamer and steam for 10 minutes. Discard the salam leaf or bay leaf before serving.

Nasi Kuning
Yellow savoury rice

This is a dish for celebrations. English people often assume that yellow rice must be Indian, but I don't think there is anything exclusively Indian about it.

Soak the rice in cold water for 1 hour, wash, and drain. Heat the oil in a saucepan and sauté the rice for 2 minutes.

Add the turmeric, coriander and cumin, stir-fry for another 2 minutes. Pour in the stock or coconut milk, and add the remaining ingredients. Simmer for about 10 minutes until the liquid has been soaked up by the rice; then steam for 10 minutes. Alternatively, cover the saucepan tightly and leave on a low heat, undisturbed, for 10 minutes. Discard the salam leaf or bay leaf before serving.

Arem-Arem
Rice stuffed with savoury chicken

Serves 6–8

FOR THE RICE
12 oz (350 g) long-grain rice
pinch of salt
2½ pints (1.4 litres) water

FOR THE FILLING
2 chicken breasts
5 shallots or 1 onion
3 cloves garlic
*3 red chillies, seeded, or ½ tsp chilli
    powder*
4 candlenuts
*½ in (1 cm) piece of shrimp paste
    (optional)*
2 tbs water
4 tbs vegetable oil
a pinch of galingale powder
1 kaffir lime leaf or bay leaf
1 tsp salt

Lovely for picnics, but equally good to serve at home as a savoury rice cake with saté or fried dishes and vegetables for a family supper. Wrap the arem-arem in banana leaves if you wish (you can usually buy them frozen, and occasionally I see fresh ones).

Boil the rice in the salted water until the water has been completely absorbed by the rice. Stir frequently to keep the rice from sticking to the bottom. Take the pan off the heat and leave to cool. The rice will be soft and sticky because it has absorbed so much water.

Simmer the chicken breasts for 40 minutes, then shred finely.

Put the shallots (or onion), garlic, chillies, candlenuts and shrimp paste into a blender with the water and half the oil and blend until smooth.

In a wok or frying pan, heat the remaining oil and fry this paste, stirring continuously, for 1 minute. Add the galingale powder, kaffir lime leaf or bay leaf and salt, stir again and add the coconut milk. Bring to the boil, and simmer for 30 minutes. Add the shredded chicken, stir for a minute or so, then continue cooking for 5–10 minutes until all the coconut milk has been absorbed by the chicken. Taste, add more salt if needed, then leave to cool.

When the rice and filling have cooled, put a third of the rice in a flameproof dish and flatten it well with the back of a spoon. Then put half of the filling on top of the rice and make it smooth and even in the same way. Then another layer of rice, then the rest of the filling, finally the rest of the rice on top.

Cover the dish, with aluminium foil if it has no lid, and steam in the oven at 180° C/350° F/Gas Mark 4 for 40–50 minutes. Serve cold, cut into squares; or, if you want to eat it hot, you can heat the cut squares in a microwave or steamer.

LEFT: *Ayam Betutu/Balinese Chicken (page 70) and Asinan Wortel Dengan Lobak/Sweet Salad of Carrots and White Radish (page 91)*

Thom Khem
Mixed stew with cellophane noodles

Serves 6–8

3½ oz (100 g) packet of cellophane
   noodles

FOR THE MEAT
4 chicken breasts
4 chicken thighs
8 oz (225 g) fillet of pork
1½ pints (900 ml) water
4 shallots, unpeeled
4 cloves garlic, unpeeled
2 tsp salt

2 tbs vegetable oil
8 oz (225 g) fresh or canned straw
   mushrooms, quartered, or 8 oz
   (225 g) fresh oyster mushrooms,
   thinly sliced
½ tsp chilli powder or ground white
   pepper
3–4 tbs dark soya sauce
1 tsp grated palm sugar or demerara
   sugar
8 oz (225 g) fresh mustard greens, or
   2 × 3½ oz (100 g) cans of
   mustard greens, roughly chopped
6 oz (175 g) fried tofu, quartered
4 hard-boiled eggs, halved
2 tbs finely chopped coriander leaves
   and stems
2 tbs finely chopped spring onions

This Thai dish reminds me of our Indonesian semur, or smoor, as the Dutch used to call it. It is an excellent way of using up leftovers of roast chicken or roast pork. In Indonesia we would make Egg Semur as a separate dish. Thom Khem has hard-boiled eggs as well as meat. I like my Thom Khem made with fresh ingredients as a family lunch or supper served with plain boiled rice. There should be plenty of sauce with it, a rich dark brown.

Soak the cellophane noodles for 3 minutes in hot water. Drain and chop them.

Put the chicken and pork in a saucepan. Pour in the water and add the whole unpeeled shallots, garlic and salt. Bring to the boil and simmer gently for 40–50 minutes, skimming several times to take the grease off the surface. Then take out the meat, shallots and garlic and allow them to cool. Strain the stock and keep for use later.

When cool, cut the chicken into bite-sized pieces, discarding the skin. Do the same for the pork. Peel the shallots and garlic and mash them on a plate with the back of a spoon.

In a wok or saucepan, heat the oil and fry the mushrooms, stirring continuously, for 1 minute. Add the mashed shallots and onions, chilli powder or pepper, soya sauce and sugar. Stir and add about 8 fl oz (200 ml) of the stock. Simmer for 4 minutes and add the mustard greens, then simmer for 2 minutes more.

Stir in the chicken, pork and fried tofu, adding more stock if needed. Simmer for 2 minutes, then add the remaining ingredients. Let this bubble for 1 minute, then serve hot.

Mie Goreng Dengan Ikan Laut
Fried noodles with seafood

Serves 4

FOR THE FRIED NOODLES
8 oz (225 g) egg noodles
2 tbs vegetable oil
5 shallots, finely chopped
1/2 tsp ground ginger
1 tsp ground coriander
2 carrots, sliced
2 cabbage leaves, coarsely shredded
2 tbs light soya sauce
2 tomatoes, peeled, seeded and chopped
4 spring onions, finely chopped
salt and pepper to taste

FOR THE STIR-FRIED SEAFOOD
8 oz (225 g) scallops
8 oz (225 g) small squid
8 oz (225 g) uncooked prawns, peeled
6 oz (175 g) any firm-fleshed fish
about 8 tbs oil
2 shallots, finely sliced
2 cloves garlic, chopped
2 tbs yellow bean sauce
a pinch of chilli powder

This is a somewhat elaborate, 'party' version of this dish. You can of course just cook the basic fried noodles, without the seafood, as the basis of a full meal or as a simple lunch by themselves.

Cook the noodles in boiling salted water for 4 minutes (or according to the instructions on the packet). Drain and rinse under running cold water for a few seconds. Loosen and shake out the strands a little, then leave to drain.

In a wok or frying pan heat the oil, and fry the shallots for 1 minute, then add the ground coriander and ginger. Stir for a few seconds, add the carrots and cabbage, continue stirring for about 4 minutes. Add the soya sauce and the noodles, and stir for 3 minutes. Add the chopped tomatoes, spring onions, and salt and pepper. Turn and stir for another minute.

Clean and prepare the scallops, squid, prawns and fish. Fry each separately in the oil in a wok or frying pan for 2–3 minutes. Discard all but 2 tablespoons of the oil used for frying the seafood. Fry the shallots and garlic in it, stirring continuously, for 2 minutes. Stir in the yellow bean sauce and a pinch of chilli powder. Add the seafood, and stir-fry all together for not more than 2 minutes. Arrange on top of the fried noodles. Serve immediately.

Miehun Goreng
Fried rice vermicelli

Serves 4

6 oz (170 g) packet rice vermicelli
1 lb (450 g) calves liver or chicken
   livers
8 oz (225 g) leeks
3 medium-sized carrots, peeled
4 oz (120 g) spring greens or mustard
   greens
2 tbs vegetable oil
1 in (2½ cm) root ginger, chopped
a pinch of chilli powder
2 tbs light soya sauce
salt to taste

Miehun Goreng is just right for a quick but nourishing lunch, whether you mix it with fish and prawns, with liver and vegetables, or with vegetables alone. Whatever you choose, the method of preparing and stir-frying the noodles and the other ingredients is the same. The recipe that follows is my own particular favourite: liver with leeks.

Put the rice vermicelli into a pan of lightly salted boiling water, cover and leave to stand for 2–3 minutes. Drain the vermicelli in a colander and run cold water from the tap over it for a few seconds. Loosen and shake out the strands of vermicelli a little, then leave to cool and dry.

Slice the liver very thin and cut into small bite-sized pieces. Cut the leeks down the middle and wash thoroughly. Then slice diagonally into pieces about ½ in (1 cm) thick. Slice the carrots diagonally as well. Wash the greens and chop them roughly.

In a wok or shallow saucepan, heat the oil. Stir-fry the leeks and carrots for 2 minutes, then add the liver, ginger and chilli powder. Stir-fry for a further 3 minutes. Add the soya sauce and greens, and continue stir-frying for another 2 minutes.

Add the vermicelli, keep on stirring and turning until all the ingredients are well mixed together and the rice vermicelli is hot. Season with salt to taste, and serve immediately.

Mee Krob
Crispy rice vermicelli

Serves 4

6 oz (170 g) packet rice vermicelli
oil for frying
2 shallots, sliced
2 cloves garlic, chopped
4 oz (120 g) pork tenderloin, coarsely
  chopped
2 chicken breasts, coarsely chopped
2 oz (60 g) shrimps
4 oz (120 g) fried beancurd, quartered
  (optional)
2 tbs yellow bean sauce
2 tbs tamarind water or 1 tbs mild
  vinegar
1 tbs sugar
2 tsp fish sauce
2 eggs, lightly beaten

FOR THE GARNISH
2 oz (60 g) beansprouts, raw or
  blanched
4 cloves pickled garlic, chopped
1 red chilli, seeded and thinly sliced
2 tbs Goreng Bawang/Fried Shallots
  (page 120)
1 tbs grated orange rind

This dish must be eaten as soon as it is cooked, and the helpings should be quite small. The meat mixture can be made well in advance, but the egg flakes must be made and mixed at the last moment. The pickled garlic can be bought in most delicatessens (usually in small jars or cans) and the grated orange rind is a substitute for som sa *(see page 20).*

Put the rice vermicelli into a pan of lightly salted boiling water. Cover the pan for 2–3 minutes. Drain the vermicelli in a colander and run cold water from the tap over it for a few seconds. Loosen and shake out the strands of vermicelli a little, then leave to drain and dry. When dry and cold, fry the vermicelli in several batches in hot oil until crisp.

In a wok or frying pan heat about 2 tbs oil, and fry the shallots and garlic for a minute or so. Add the pork and chicken and stir-fry for 3 minutes. Then add the shrimps, beancurd (if used), yellow bean sauce and tamarind water. Stir again, and simmer for 3 minutes. Add the sugar and fish sauce, and leave to simmer gently while you fry the egg.

In a frying pan, heat about 4 tbs oil. With a spoon, dribble the beaten egg continually into the oil; each drop will become a golden flake. Stir and remove with a slotted spoon.

Just before serving, mix the crisp vermicelli with the meat mixture and the egg flakes in a large wok over a medium heat. Mix and stir for about 2 minutes. This can be done in stages, a portion at a time, if the wok is too small to take it all at once. Garnish and serve immediately.

Sen Mee Pud
Rice-stick noodles with pork and beansprouts

Serves 4

6–8 oz (175–225 g) rice-stick noodles
  or udon
2 tbs peanut oil or vegetable oil
2 shallots, thinly sliced
1 in (2½ cm) piece of root ginger,
  finely chopped
2 green chillies, seeded and sliced
  diagonally
2 cloves garlic, crushed
1 tbs light soya sauce
1 tbs fish sauce
6 oz (175 g) roast pork, thinly sliced
4 spring onions, sliced diagonally
4 oz (120 g) beansprouts
2 tbs chopped coriander leaves
salt and sugar to taste

See page 18 for a description of rice-stick noodles. For this recipe, I often use Japanese noodles called udon. *It's a good dish for finishing off the leftovers of Sunday roast pork, crackling and all.*

Boil the noodles in lightly salted water for 4–5 minutes, or according to the instructions on the packet. Wash in a colander under a running cold tap for a few seconds, then leave to drain and cool.

In a wok or large saucepan, heat the oil. Fry the shallots, chopped ginger, green chillies and garlic for 2 minutes, stirring continuously. Add the soya sauce and fish sauce. Stir-fry for 2 more minutes. Add the pork and spring onions, simmer for 2 minutes, then add the beansprouts and chopped coriander leaves. Stir-fry for a further 2 minutes. Taste and add salt and sugar.

Stir in the noodles and serve immediately. If you have some leftover crackling, break it up into small pieces and sprinkle over the noodles.

VEGETABLES, TOFU
AND TEMPEH

I am sometimes tempted to turn vegetarian when I consider how many good things can be made with vegetables alone. With tofu and tempeh, after all, one need not worry about missing any vital proteins or vitamins. I can't quite bring myself yet to abandon a whole area of cooking and eating, but it is certainly no hardship for me to cater for a vegetarian party. Most of the dishes in this section are very lightly cooked, so the ingredients keep their flavour and texture as well as their goodness. Don't assume, however, that this means you needn't start doing anything about the meal until just before you want to eat. Thai and Indonesian food takes, as a rule, much longer to prepare than it does to cook; there is a lot of cleaning and cutting-up to be done.

Tofu and tempeh are both made from soya beans. Tofu, bean curd (tahu in Indonesian), is quite familiar in western countries now; you can buy it fresh, in which case you submerge it in water and keep it in the fridge for, at most, 3 or 4 days; or you can buy packets of 'everlasting' or 'silken' tofu, which is good but a little too soft to be ideal for my purposes; or you can buy kits and make your own. Buying the fresh tofu is really the best.

Tempeh is not yet well-known in Britain, though it is available in most health-food shops in the United States and of course in Holland, where the links with Indonesia are still in some respects remarkably close. The Thais don't know anything about tempeh, and many regions of Indonesia itself don't make it and don't like it – my father, who was born and raised in West Sumatra, would never touch it. But the Javanese love it, and as I spent so much of my early life in Java I became fond of it too. Some health-food shops in Britain stock it; several small firms in this country make it, and at least one Dutch factory makes it in quantity and exports it. The best and freshest tempeh is the tempeh you make yourself; see the bibliography for details of Bill and Akiko Shurtleff's excellent *Book of Tempeh*.

Bamboo shoot, peppers and chilli, diamond-shaped bamboo shoot cuttings

Oseng-Oseng Tauge Dan Ercis
Stir-fried beansprouts and mange-tout

Serves 4

1 lb (450 g) beansprouts
2 tbs sunflower oil
2 shallots, thinly sliced
1 clove garlic, crushed
1 in (2½ cm) root ginger, finely
  chopped
a pinch of chilli powder or ground
  white pepper
1 tbs light soya sauce
8 oz (225 g) mange-tout, topped and
  tailed
½ tsp salt
a large pinch of sugar

This is a dish that is delicious, attractive and very easy and quick to make. It is an everyday dish in Indonesia, as both the main ingredients are relatively cheap to buy and are available all year round.

I usually pick off and discard the brownish roots of the beansprouts, which is a very time-consuming job but will make your dish look much more attractive. However, it is sufficient to clean the beansprouts as follows: put them in a large bowl, run a cold tap over the bowl, fill it full and then carefully tip the water out. By doing this several times you will get rid of the green bits of the mung beans that stuck to the sprouts.

In a wok or large frying pan, heat the oil and fry the shallots, garlic and ginger for 1 minute, stirring all the time. Add the chilli powder or pepper and the soya sauce. Stir, then add the mange-tout. Stir for 1 minute and add the beansprouts. Continue stirring for 2 minutes, then add the salt and sugar and stir again. Serve immediately, or eat cold as a salad.

Jukut Murab
Black-eye beans in coconut dressing

Serves 6–8

1 lb (450 g) black-eye beans
2 tsp fried shrimp paste (optional)
1 coconut, freshly grated
4 spring onions, thinly sliced
1 large red chilli, seeded
½ tsp chilli powder
2 cloves garlic, crushed
juice of 1 lime
1 tsp soft brown sugar
1 tsp salt
1 cucumber, thinly sliced
2 tbs chopped mint or basil

This is a Balinese version of a salad, popular all over Java, which makes good use of young and tender coconut for the dressing. Even though the fresh coconuts available in the west are quite old and a bit tough and chewy, you'll be surprised how good this spicy coconut dressing is. If you are a vegetarian this recipe is just made for you.

Soak the black-eye beans in cold water overnight. Wash and drain, then boil them in lightly salted water for 40–50 minutes. Drain again.

Put the shrimp paste (if used) in a bowl, and mash it with a wooden spoon. Add the remaining ingredients, except the beans, the cucumber and the mint or basil. Mix well, then add these final ingredients. Mix together thoroughly, and serve as a cold salad.

Urap Kol
Steamed cabbage in coconut dressing

Serves 4–6

1 lb (450 g) white cabbage, finely
    shredded
2 tsp fried shrimp paste
2 cloves garlic, crushed
juice of 1 lime
1/2 tsp chilli powder
1 tsp soft brown sugar (optional)
1 tsp salt
1 coconut, freshly grated

In Indonesia we consider this an everyday, family dish. I have served it at dinner parties in London, however, where it was regarded as rather exotic. No doubt it was the coconut (freshly grated) that did it.

Steam the shredded cabbage for 3 minutes. Keep warm.

Put the fried shrimp paste on a plate and mash it with the back of a spoon. Add the crushed garlic, lime juice, chilli powder, sugar (if used) and salt. Mix well. Then add this paste mixture to the grated coconut. Mix well again, adding more salt if necessary.

Dress the steamed cabbage with the coconut dressing, and serve warm or cold.

Asinan Wortel Dengan Lobak
Sweet salad of carrots and white radish

Serves 4–6

8 oz (225 g) carrots
8 oz (225 g) white radish
3 tbs white distilled vinegar
5 tbs warm water
1 tbs caster sugar
1 tsp salt
1 red chilli, seeded and thinly sliced or
    a pinch of chilli powder
1 green chilli, seeded and thinly sliced
2 shallots, thinly sliced

This is a simple but very refreshing salad, just as good with a snack (especially fried snacks) as it is when you serve it with your main course.

Cut the carrots and radishes into very fine matchsticks.

Mix the vinegar, water, sugar and salt. Beat with a fork until the sugar and salt dissolve. Add all the other ingredients, and mix well.

This salad will keep in the fridge for 2–3 days. It is equally good if you substitute beansprouts for the white radishes; you then have Asinan Wortel Dengan Taugé.

Pecel

Mixed cooked vegetable salad with peanut sauce

Serves 4–6

FOR THE SAUCE
4 fl oz (120 ml) vegetable oil
4 oz (120 g) raw peanuts
1 clove garlic, finely chopped
2 shallots, thinly sliced
1/2 in (1 cm) piece of shrimp paste
salt
1/2 teaspoon chilli powder
1/2 teaspoon brown sugar
3/4 pint (450 ml) water
juice of 1/2 a lemon

4 oz (120 g) cabbage or spring greens,
*   shredded*
4 oz (120 g) French beans, cut into 2
*   or 3*
4 oz (120 g) carrots, thinly sliced into
*   rounds*
4 oz (120 g) cauliflower, cut into
*   florets*
4 oz (120 g) beansprouts (optional)

Pecel is pronounced p'tsh'l – an Indonesian c is like ch in church. As a dish, it is similar to the better-known Gado-Gado, but simpler. Since it is regarded simply as a vegetable dish to accompany your rice meal, it is not normally garnished, as Gado-Gado would be if served as a complete lunch.

Heat the oil in a frying pan, and fry the peanuts for 4 minutes. Remove with a slotted spoon to drain in a colander. Leave to cool. Pound or grind the peanuts into a fine powder, using a blender, coffee grinder or pestle and mortar. Discard the oil except for 1 tablespoonful.

Crush the garlic, shallots and shrimp paste in a mortar, with a little salt. Fry in the remaining oil for 1 minute. Add the chilli powder, sugar, more salt and the water. Bring to the boil, and stir in the ground peanuts. Simmer for 4–6 minutes, stirring occasionally, until the sauce becomes thick. Add the lemon juice and set aside to use later.

Boil each vegetable separately for 3–4 minutes. Drain and arrange on a serving plate. Heat the sauce and pour over the vegetables. Serve hot or warm.

If necessary, this can be prepared and mixed together in advance, then heated in a microwave for 1–2 minutes on full power.

Terung Isi
Stuffed aubergines

Serves 4 as a starter

2 large or 4 medium-sized aubergines
2 tbs salt
8 oz (225 g) pea aubergines or okra, or
* 1 medium-sized aubergine*
vegetable oil for deep frying
2 tbs olive oil
2 medium-sized onions, sliced
4 cloves garlic, finely chopped
2 red or green chillies, seeded and cut
* diagonally*
2 tsp roasted coriander seeds
1 tsp black peppercorns
2 fresh kaffir lime leaves, shredded, or
* dried kaffir lime leaves, crushed*
a pinch of galingale powder
1 tbs tamarind water or lemon juice
2 tsp brown sugar (optional)
salt to taste
4 tbs chopped flat-leaved parsley or curly
* parsley*

Several different kinds of aubergine grow in Indonesia and Thailand, and each country has its own favourite ways of cooking them. In Indonesia we often stuff them with minced lamb. However, I once had to devise a big dinner which was entirely vegetarian, and I used small 'pea' aubergines to stuff the big ones. This was very succcessful.

Halve the aubergines lengthwise. Make 2 deep slashes, lengthwise then crosswise, on the exposed surface of each half. Sprinkle these liberally with the salt. Put them in a colander upside down; leave for 30–50 minutes, then wash the salt away under the cold tap. Pat the aubergines dry with kitchen paper before deep frying them. If, in addition, you are using the whole aubergine instead of pea aubergines or okra, cut into julienne strips, sprinkle the strips also with salt, leave for 30–50 minutes, wash and drain.

If using pea aubergines, take off the stalk and wash, then put in a colander to drain. If using okra, wash and cut them into 3–4 pieces.

In a wok or large frying pan heat the vegetable oil. When smoke rises, fry the half-aubergines 2 at a time, for 3 minutes each time, turning them once. Keep on kitchen paper to drain off as much oil as possible. When all the aubergine halves are fried, fry the julienne strips of aubergine in the same oil for 2 minutes, stirring all the time. Remove with a slotted spoon to drain. Now, with a spoon, carefully so as not to damage the skin, scoop out the flesh from the aubergine halves, chop roughly and keep aside.

Discard the oil and wipe the wok or frying pan to remove the bits of aubergine. Add the 2 tbs olive oil, heat, and fry the onions, stirring continuously, for 3 minutes. Add the garlic, chillies, ground coriander, pepper, kaffir lime leaves and galingale powder. Stir, and add the chopped aubergine flesh and strips, or the pea-aubergines or okra. Continue cooking, stirring all the time. Now add salt, tamarind water or lemon juice, and sugar. Keep stirring and turning for about 2 minutes and lastly add the chopped parsley, mixing it well into the aubergines. Take off the stove.

Divide the filling into 4 or 8, and fill the aubergine halves. Arrange in an ovenproof dish, and cook in the oven at 180° C/350° F/Gas Mark 4 for 30–40 minutes. Serve hot or cold.

Tahu Isi Sayuran
Stuffed beancurd

Serves 4

FOR THE STUFFING
3 medium-sized carrots
2 oz (60 g) mange-tout
4 oz (120 g) oyster mushrooms or
  other mushrooms
1 tbs vegetable oil
2 spring onions, thinly sliced
2 cloves garlic, thinly sliced
4 oz (120 g) beansprouts
salt and pepper to taste
1 packet (8 oz/225 g, about 16–18
  pieces) fried tofu

FOR THE SAUCE
3 cloves garlic
4 ripe, red tomatoes
1 tbs vegetable oil
3 shallots, thinly sliced
1 in (2½ cm) root ginger, finely
  chopped
a pinch of chilli powder
½ tsp ground coriander
1 tbs light soya sauce
salt and sugar to taste

FOR THE GARNISH
1 yellow pepper, seeded and cut into
  diamond shapes, blanched
2 oz (60 g) mange-tout, blanched

RIGHT: *Dok Mai Khai Nok Kra Ta/
Quail Egg 'Flowers' (page 104), Popia
Tawt/Fried Miniature Spring Rolls (page
28), Nam Chim/Sweet and Sour Chilli
Sauce (page 124) and Kratong Thong/
Golden Cups with lettuce-leaf variation
(page 102)*

Indonesian stuffed beancurd is usually stuffed with minced chicken and prawns, but here I have described a vegetarian dish, using a stuffing of mixed vegetables.

Fried tofu becomes moist and soft in a sauce and absorbs the flavour of the sauce most deliciously. This stuffed beancurd, therefore, is particularly good if you steam it in the sauce, or simmer it with the sauce in a saucepan. I have chosen a simple tomato sauce, garnished with yellow peppers and mange-tout for colour.

To make the stuffing, cut the carrots, mange-tout and mushrooms into short, thin matchsticks. Heat the oil in a wok or saucepan, add the spring onions and garlic, stir-fry for 2 minutes, add the beansprouts and vegetables and continue stir-frying for about 2 minutes more. Season with salt and pepper. Leave to cool.

With a pair of scissors, cut one side off each tofu cake but do not remove it completely. Scoop out the white tofu from inside with a spoon, chop, and mix with the vegetables.

Divide the vegetable filling among the tofu cubes. Close them, and arrange in a large saucepan or on a dish that will fit inside your steamer.

To make the sauce, put the garlic in a saucepan of water that is just boiling; simmer for 5 minutes, add the whole tomatoes and simmer for another 5 minutes. In a small saucepan, heat the oil and fry the sliced shallots for a few minutes. Add the ginger, stir for a minute, and add the chilli powder and ground coriander. Then sieve the tomatoes and garlic into the pan. Stir, add the soya sauce, and season with salt and sugar.

Pour the sauce over the stuffed tofu, and finally simmer for 5–6 minutes. Serve hot, garnished with blanched yellow peppers and mange-tout.

Yam Mamuang
Thai mango salad with pork

Serves 4–6

FOR THE MANGO SALAD
2 large half-ripe mangoes, cut into
   julienne strips
1/2 tsp salt
1 tbs sugar
juice of 1 lime or lemon

FOR THE MEAT
2 tbs peanut oil
8 oz (225 g) fillet of pork, cut into
   julienne strips
2 shallots, thinly sliced
2 cloves garlic, chopped
3 tbs fish sauce
1 tbs mild vinegar
4 spring onions, thinly sliced
2 dried red chillies, seeded and coarsely
   chopped, or 1/2 tsp chilli powder or
   ground white pepper
3 tbs roasted peanuts, coarsely crushed
salt to taste

In Indonesia a fruit salad like this would not be mixed with meat. I tasted a mango salad with meat in Bangkok, and liked it very much. If you are a vegetarian you can of course leave out the meat. The best mangoes for this dish are half-ripe ones, still hard but already turning yellow.

Put the mango strips into a bowl with the salt, sugar and lime or lemon juice. Mix well.

In a wok or frying pan, heat the oil and fry the strips of pork, stirring continuously, for 3 minutes. Take out with a slotted spoon and put aside on some absorbent paper.

In the same oil, fry the shallots and garlic for 1 minute, and add the fish sauce, vinegar, spring onions and chopped chillies or chilli powder. Stir and add the mangoes and pork; stir again and remove from the heat. Put everything into a bowl, add the crushed peanuts and salt to taste, and mix well. Allow to cool, then chill in the refrigerator and serve cold.

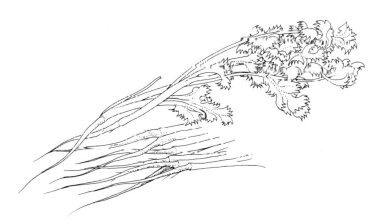

LEFT: *Agar Delima Serikaya/
Pomegranate and Coconut Cream Agar-
Agar (page 110) and Indonesian
Cinnamon Layer Cake (page 113)*

Ketoprak
Beancurd salad

Serves 2

4 fl oz (250 ml) peanut oil
2 cakes beancurd, each cut into 6
  pieces
4 oz (120 g) beansprouts
salt to taste
2 medium-sized potatoes, peeled and
  thinly sliced
¼ cucumber, peeled and sliced
2 tbs chopped flat-leaved parsley
8 tbs (more if desired) Sambal
  Kacang/Peanut Sauce (page 122)
8–10 emping crackers (page 125)
1 tbs Goreng Bawang/Fried Shallots
  (page 120)

This is a favourite lunch dish in Central Java. You can find it in many small warungs, open-sided cafés where young students gather because the food is good and cheap.

In a non-stick frying pan heat the oil and fry the beancurd for about 5 minutes, turning them over once. Remove with slotted spoon and drain in a colander.

Clean the beansprouts and put them in a bowl. Pour over them boiling water with a little salt. Cover and leave for 3 minutes, then drain and keep them warm. Fry the thinly sliced potatoes until crisp.

To serve, arrange the fried beancurd on serving plates with the fried potatoes, slices of cucumber and beansprouts. Top with the chopped flat-leaved parsley. Pour over this as much sauce as you like, crush or break the emping over it, and sprinkle on some fried shallots or onions as well.

SNACKS AND SWEETS

This section covers food for picnics and meals on journeys as well as cocktail snacks and the occasional light lunch and of course some sweet things that will round off a meal. I cannot say, in all honesty, that South-East Asian cuisines are as distinguished for sweets as they are for savoury dishes. The Javanese (to take just one example) have a sweet tooth and consume huge amounts of sugar, probably far more than is good for them, but they have never evolved a large repertoire of sweets or puddings and their confectioners' shops and pâtisseries rely heavily on Dutch traditions and recipes. Nevertheless, there are some good things that deserve to be included here.

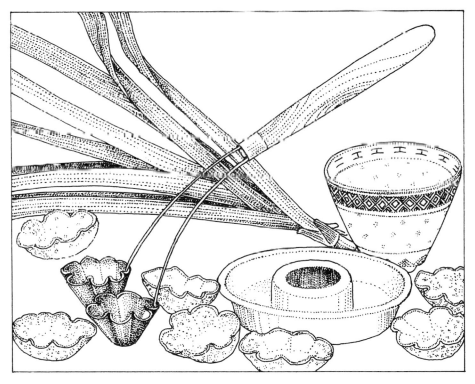

Kratong thong scoop, ready made kratong thong, pandanus leaf, putu manis cups

Kratong Thong
Golden cups

Makes 50–60 'cups'

FOR THE 'CUPS' BATTER
4 oz (120 g) rice flour or plain flour
2 tsp olive oil
6 fl oz (170 ml) cold water
1/2 tsp salt
1/2 tsp caster sugar
vegetable oil for deep frying

FOR THE FILLING
3 oz (90 g) roasted unsalted peanuts
2 tbs vegetable oil
1 large onion, finely chopped
3 cloves garlic, finely chopped
1 lb (450 g) boneless chicken breast,
    minced or finely chopped
a pinch of chilli powder or ground
    white pepper
2 tbs finely chopped coriander stalks
2 tbs finely chopped coriander leaves
1 tsp salt
1/2 tsp sugar
2 tsp light soya sauce
2 tsp fish sauce (optional)
1 oz (30 g) roasted unsalted peanuts,
    roughly chopped

FOR THE GARNISH
1 tbs chopped coriander leaves
4–6 small red chillies, seeded and
    finely chopped

See page 101 for the drawing of the kratong thong scoop or mould, which as far as I know at the time of writing is not available in London. I bought mine in Bangkok. However, ready-made kratong thong 'cups' are often available in Thai shops, packed in tens or twenties in airtight cellophane bags. If you cannot buy them and do not want to make them, puff pastry vol-au-vents will do very well instead; the really special thing here is the filling.

I recently tasted the most delicious kratong thong fillings served on crispy lettuce leaves at Franco and Ann Taruschio's famous Walnut Tree Restaurant near Abergavenny in Wales. Everything was just right: the minced pork, the peanuts, coriander stalks and chilli. On the menu they were described as a 'Thai pork appetizer'. Served as a first course the lettuce leaves are ideal, but as party snacks the cups are more practical. The cups can be made in advance. My recipe was given to me by a good friend in Bangkok; it uses chicken instead of pork. The rest of the ingredients will be the same for either meat.

Put the flour in a bowl. Make a well in the middle, pour in the olive oil and start mixing the oil and flour with a wooden spoon while gradually adding the water. Mix vigorously until all the water is used. Add the salt and sugar and mix again.

The best way to make the golden cups is to use a deep fryer with a thermostat because you need to keep the oil temperature between 180°–200° C (350°–400°F). Heat the oil to this temperature and put the kratong thong scoop in the oil for about 4 minutes. Dip the outside of the hot scoop up to the brim in the batter and leave it there for 10 seconds. Don't let any batter overflow into the scoop. A layer of batter will start to cook and will adhere to the bottom of the scoop. Now plunge the scoop into the hot oil. Hold it there for 10 seconds before shaking the batter 'cups' off the scoop. (You may need to give them a push with a spoon to free them.) Now you have 2 nice golden cups. Remove with a slotted spoon to drain on a plate lined with kitchen paper.

Continue as before until all the batter has been used up. This batter will make about 50–60 golden cups. When cool store in airtight container for later use. They will keep crisp for about 1 week provided the container is really airtight.

To make the filling, chop the roasted unsalted peanuts the same size as the chicken. Heat the oil in a wok or large frying pan, and fry the onions and garlic, stirring all the time, until they are soft. Add the chicken, chilli powder and coriander stalks, stir-fry for about 3 minutes, then add the remaining ingredients except the peanuts.

Continue cooking, stirring occasionally, for 4 minutes. Add the roughly chopped peanuts and stir continuously for 1 minute. Adjust the seasoning and leave to cool. Just before serving fill the cups and sprinkle with the garnish.

To serve as a starter, pile about 2 tablespoons of this filling on top of a crispy lettuce leaf. Serve 3 of these per person. Leave out the chopped chillies in the garnish if you don't like it hot.

Dok Mai Khai Nok Kra Ta
Quail egg 'flowers'

Makes 12 'flowers'

6 small cucumbers or 12 radishes
12 quail eggs

FOR THE MARINADE
8 fl oz (250 ml) water
2 tbs vinegar
1/2 tsp salt
2 tbs sugar

TO COLOUR THE EGGS
1 tbs chopped coriander root
2 cloves garlic, chopped
1 tbs vegetable oil
a pinch of ground white pepper
a pinch of salt
1 tbs sugar
4 tbs dark soya sauce

12 cocktail sticks

The Thais usually make these with miniature cucumbers, about as big as large gherkins. In fact, gherkins can take the place of the cucumbers very well; or I sometimes use round radishes, which are easy to cut into 'flowers'. With a little practice, you can cut flowers out of carrots, chillies and many other vegetables. Quail egg flowers do take a little time to prepare, but if you are as fond of quail eggs as I must admit I am, then the time is well spent.

Cut the radishes, or whatever vegetables you use to make the 'flowers', into shape. Putting the cut shapes into iced water often makes them 'open' further.

If you use small cucumbers, cut them in half, hollow them out to a depth of about 1 in (2½ cm), and cut the thin sides into petal shapes. Mix together the marinade ingredients, add the cucumbers or radishes and marinate for 30 minutes.

Meanwhile, boil the quail eggs in salted water for 4 minutes. Drain and peel.

In a frying pan, fry the chopped coriander root and garlic in the oil for 1 minute. Add the pepper, salt, sugar and soya sauce. Stir for another minute. Strain through a sieve into a small bowl. Put the eggs in and marinate for about 2 minutes, turning them several times until they are all evenly brown.

Put each egg into the petals of a cucumber flower, and pierce with a cocktail stick 'stem' to hold them together.

Pergedel Jagung Dengan Terung
Sweet corn fritters with aubergine

Makes 15–18 fritters

6 fresh corn cobs or 11½ oz (326 g)
  can sweetcorn
1 medium-sized aubergine
salt
vegetable oil
4 shallots, chopped
1 red chilli, seeded and chopped or
  ½ tsp chilli powder
2 cloves garlic, chopped
1 tsp ground coriander
3 tbs rice flour or plain flour
1 tsp baking powder
2 tbs chopped spring onions
1 large egg

This is a delicious snack, very easy to make, and as good for picnics as it is for parties. Some people prefer them hot, others cold, but I have never met anyone who doesn't want more.

If you are using fresh corn, grate the corn off the cobs. If canned sweetcorn is used, drain and put into a bowl, then mash it a little with a wooden spoon just to break the kernels so they won't pop when fried. Or you can put them in a blender and blend for a few seconds.

Cut the aubergine into very small cubes, put them in a colander and sprinkle generously with salt. Leave for 30 minutes–1 hour, rinse off the salt and squeeze the excess water out. Heat 2 tbs oil in a wok or frying pan, and fry the shallots, chilli and garlic, stirring them for a minute or so. Then add the aubergines, stir, and season with ground coriander and salt. Simmer, stirring often, for 4 minutes. Take off the heat and leave to cool.

When cool, add the aubergine mixture to the mashed sweet corn with the flour, baking powder and chopped spring onions. Mix thoroughly and add the egg. Mix well again, taste, and add more salt if necessary.

In a frying-pan, heat 5 tbs oil. Drop a heaped tablespoon of the mixture into the pan. Flatten it with a fork, and repeat this process until you have 5 or 6 pergedel in the pan. Fry them for about 3 minutes on each side, turning once. Serve hot or cold as a snack or as finger food at a party.

Tod Man (Pla Krai)
Savoury fish cakes

2 lb (1 kg) white fish (angler fish or
  cod), diced

FOR THE MARINADE
5 shallots, chopped
4 cloves garlic, chopped
3 red chillies, seeded and chopped
4 coriander roots, chopped
4 fresh kaffir lime leaves, shredded or
  dried kaffir lime leaves, crushed
2 oz (60 g) yard-long beans or French
  beans, sliced into thin rounds
2 tsp sugar
2 tsp light soya sauce
1/2 tsp salt
1/4 tsp pepper
2 tbs olive oil

vegetable oil for deep frying

This is sometimes spelt Tod Mun. Some add the name of the fish it is most often made with in Thailand, and call it Tod Man Pla Krai. Pla krai is a common freshwater fish, and Tod Man is everyday food, but delicious. My recipe was given to me by one of the Thai chefs whom I met when I spent a fortnight as a guest cook at the Inter-Continental Hotel at Hyde Park Corner. This, then, is Chef Mongkol Puntar's Tod Man, except that I use less coriander root than he does.

Mix all the marinade ingredients with the fish in a bowl. Leave to marinate for 30–40 minutes, or overnight in the fridge.

Mince the marinated fish in a meat mincer or food processor.

Take about 1 tbs of the fish, put it on the palm of your hand and form it into a ball. Make all the fish into fish balls in the same way. Everything up to this point can be done a day or two in advance and the fish balls stored in the fridge.

To cook, flatten the fish balls by pressing them gently on a flat surface. Then deep-fry 5 or 6 at a time for 2–3 minutes in a wok or deep-fryer. Take out with a slotted spoon and drain on kitchen paper. Serve hot or warm as a snack with drinks.

Bakwan Ikan
Beansprout and fish fritters

Makes about 20 fritters

8 oz (250 g) fish, chopped
8 oz (250 g) beansprouts
4 oz (120 g) rice flour or plain flour
2 tsp baking powder
1 tsp ground coriander
a pinch of turmeric
2 red or green chillies, seeded and
    finely chopped
4 spring onions, thinly sliced
3 cloves garlic, finely chopped
1 in (2½ cm) root ginger, chopped
1 tsp light soya sauce
1 tsp salt
2 small eggs, beaten
oil for deep frying

Bakwan is one of the many snacks that hawkers sell from house to house in almost every town in Java. They pass your house several times during the day, each with his characteristic cry.

This is my version of Bakwan, somewhat lighter than the hawkers sell. I love making these for drinks parties; everyone says they are 'moreish'. Any boneless fish flesh can be used, but my favourite is salmon. Leftover cuts or trimmings from salmon fillets are perfect for this recipe.

In a bowl, mix together all the ingredients, except the oil. Heat the oil in a chip pan or wok to 180° C/350° F. With a fork, pick up a little of the batter and drop it into the hot oil. Do this 6 or 8 times, frying each for about 3 minutes.

Remove the fritters with a slotted spoon, put to drain on absorbent paper. Repeat this process until all the batter has been used up. Serve hot or cold. Can also be served with Nam Chim/Sweet and Sour Chilli Sauce (page 124) as a dip.

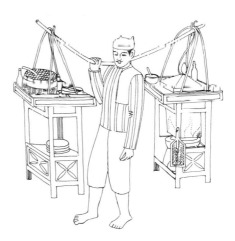

Martabak Isi Ayam Dan Rebung

Savoury pancakes with chicken and bamboo shoot filling

Makes about 20 pancakes

FOR THE CASING
*1 packet (4 oz/120 g) wonton
  wrappers*

FOR THE FILLING
1 tbs olive oil or corn oil
2 large onions, thinly sliced
2 cloves garlic, crushed
1 tsp ground coriander
½ tsp ground cumin
*1 tsp ground ginger or chopped fresh
  ginger*
*1 tsp chilli powder or freshly ground
  black pepper*
½ tsp turmeric
*1 tsp lemon grass powder or 2 in
  (5 cm) fresh lemon grass, finely
  chopped*
1 lb (450 g) chicken meat, minced
*4 oz (120 g) canned bamboo shoots,
  diced very small*
salt
3 eggs, beaten
4 spring onions, thinly sliced

5 tbs olive oil or corn oil for frying

These are not strictly pancakes at all; they are envelopes of very thin dough, stuffed with minced meat and spices and then quickly fried. The original Martabak from India has minced beef or minced lamb filling. My version here is filled with chicken and bamboo shoots. They can accompany a meal, or be served with drinks, or you can eat one any time as a snack.

Heat 1 tablespoon oil in a wok or frying pan and fry the onions and garlic until soft. Add the spices, fry for another half-minute, stirring all the time, then stir in the minced chicken and bamboo shoots. Fry, stirring occasionally, for about 15 minutes. Season with salt. Let the mixture cool for 30 minutes–1 hour. Put the mixture in a bowl, add the beaten eggs and the spring onions. Mix well.

To fill the martabak, lay out a few wonton skins on a pastry board. Put a tablespoon of filling into half of each wonton square. Then fold the other half over the filling and press the edges down so that they are more or less sealed.

Heat the oil in a frying pan to a high temperature. Fry the filled martabak, 5–6 at a time, for about 2 minutes each side: turn once only. The casing should be quite crisp around the edges, but not in the middle, and the finished martabak should be flat and evenly filled with meat almost to the edge. Serve hot or cold.

Rempeyek Kacang Hijau
Mung beans savoury crisps

Makes 50–60 savoury crisps

4 oz (120 g) mung beans, soaked
  overnight
2 candlenuts
1 clove garlic
2 tsp ground coriander
1 tsp salt
4 oz (120 g) rice powder
8 fl oz (250 ml) cold water
peanut oil or sunflower oil for frying

I don't think you can find a more delicious crisp than this Indonesian rempeyek. At first glance you might think the recipe is difficult to make, but I assure you it is not at all tricky. One point to remember is that you need the oriental rice powder for this, as the rice flour you get at the supermarket is not fine enough.

Drain the mung beans.

Pound the candlenuts and garlic together and add the coriander and the salt. Mix in the rice powder, then add the water, a little at a time, stirring and mixing thoroughly. Add the mung beans to the batter.

To fry rempeyek, you need a non-stick frying pan and a wok. Heat some oil in the frying pan, and enough in the wok to deep-fry the rempeyek. Take 1 tablespoon of the batter, with some beans in it, and pour it quickly into the frying-pan. Fry it there for 1–2 minutes – you will probably be able to do 6–7 rempeyek at a time – and then drop the half-cooked rempeyek into the hot oil in the wok. Deep-fry them until they are crisp and golden: this will take a few minutes. Carry on like this until all the batter and the beans are used up. Drain and allow to go cold.

Store in an airtight container for up to 2 weeks.

Agar Delima Serikaya
Pomegranate and coconut cream agar-agar

Serves 4

2 oz (60 g) agar-agar strands, soaked
   in water
2 ripe pomegranates
4 tbs cold water
5 tbs caster sugar
3 eggs
4 fl oz (120 ml) coconut cream (see
   p. 16)
a pinch of salt
2 pints (1.1 litres) cold water

Delima *(pronounced* d'lee-ma) *is the Indonesian name for pomegranate. A ripe one, when you open it, has deep pink or ruby-coloured seeds which are very juicy. Agar-agar (in names of dishes often shortened simply to agar) is extracted from various species of seaweed* (Eucheuma, Gracilaria, Gelidium). *It will gell even without refrigeration, so it is ideal for use in the tropics. It has no taste of its own, so feel free to experiment with different ingredients. I have chosen for you here what is, in my opinion, the most delicious and finest-looking agar dish.*

Keep the agar-agar strands soaked in water while you are preparing the rest of the ingredients. To open the pomegranates, make a deep short slash in the middle of the fruit with a sharp knife, then with both hands press the fruit hard, and it will break open completely. Now take out the seeds by hand, carefully, so you don't squeeze the juice out. Collect the seeds in a bowl. I don't advise you to squeeze the juice with a lemon squeezer because the yellow membrane surrounding the seeds produces a bitter liquid. Be careful also; this liquid will leave a brown stain on cloth that nothing will shift. Therefore, discard the membrane.

Set aside a few seeds for decoration and put the rest in a small saucepan, add the 4 tbs water and 1 tbs of the caster sugar. Bring to the boil and simmer for 2 minutes. Pass through a fine sieve lined with muslin and squeeze as much juice as you can into a bowl. Set aside to cool.

Break the eggs into a bowl and beat with a wire whisk until frothy. Add the coconut cream, whisk to mix, then add the salt and the remaining sugar. Heat this mixture, preferably in a double saucepan, stirring continuously, for about 4 minutes or until the mixture is thick. This has now become the serikaya. Set aside.

Drain and rinse the agar-agar strands. Put them in a saucepan with the water, bring to the boil and simmer, stirring occasionally, until the agar-agar has dissolved. Strain the liquid into a measuring jug, then put half into the bowl with the pomegranate juice and the other half into the serikaya bowl. Stir the contents of each bowl vigorously with a wooden spoon.

Pour the pomegranate agar into the chosen mould and chill for a few minutes, while you continue stirring the serikaya. Take out the pomegranate agar from the fridge, pour the serikaya on top, and chill until needed.

Sankhaya
Steamed custard in peaches or nectarines

Serves 6

6 peaches or nectarines
3 eggs
6 tbs grated palm sugar
a pinch of salt
6 fl oz (150 ml) very thick coconut milk

Sankhaya is the Thai name for what in Indonesia is called Serikaya. The Thais, and (I believe) the Laotians, pour the sankhaya into a seeded but whole pumpkin, steam the pumpkin, and serve it cold, cut into slices. This is delicious, but it is equally good with peaches or nectarines, and much easier to make.

Halve the peaches or nectarines and remove the stones. Scoop out a little of the flesh.

Beat the eggs lightly, add the sugar, a pinch of salt and the coconut milk and stir until the sugar is dissolved.

Three-quarters fill the peaches or nectarines with the custard and put them carefully in a heatproof dish. Steam for 10–15 minutes. To be eaten cold.

Kue Lapis
Layered steamed rice-flour cake

Makes 1 × 8 inch (20 cm) cake

2 pandanus leaves, fresh or frozen
4 tbs cold water
1½ pints (900 ml) very thick coconut milk
a pinch of salt
4 oz (120 g) caster sugar
8 oz (225 g) rice flour
3½ oz (100 g) cornflour

Like Lapis Legit/Indonesian Cinnamon Layer Cake (page 113), this steamed cake is time-consuming to make. However, it looks exotic, is very cheap to make and tastes delicious. I recommend it especially for a large buffet party, although you can make a small Kue Lapis as well. In Indonesia you can buy Kue Lapis from street vendors who specialise in them, and we eat slices as a snack at any time. The usual colours are green and white, often with layers of red as well.

To make the pandanus juice: put the leaves and water in a blender. Blend for a few seconds, then pass through a fine sieve into a bowl. You will now have about 3 tablespoons of green, fragrant liquid.

In a saucepan heat the coconut milk, salt and sugar, almost to boiling point, stirring to dissolve the sugar. Remove from heat and leave to cool a little. Sift the rice flour and cornflour into a bowl. Gradually pour in lukewarm coconut milk, stirring until you get a smooth, thickish batter. Divide this batter between 2 bowls, and put the pandanus juice into one of them. Stir until you get an even green colour.

Heat a steamer or a double saucepan. When the water in the bottom pan is boiling, heat an 8 in (20 cm) cake tin for 2 minutes. Pour in the white batter to make a layer about ¼ in (5 mm) thick or less. Steam for 2 minutes, then add the same thickness of the green batter and steam for 2 minutes, then add more layers alternately.

When all the batter is used up, cover and continue cooking for 3–4 minutes. Cool the cake slightly before turning out onto a plate. When cold cut into about 20 small, thin slices. Serve at teatime or with coffee after dinner.

Lapis Legit
Indonesian cinnamon layer cake

Makes 1 × 8–9 inch (20–25 cm) cake

1 lb (450 g) unsalted butter
drop of vanilla essence
8 oz (225 g) caster sugar
16–19 egg yolks (size 2)
3 tbs top of the milk
5 oz (150 g) plain flour
a pinch of salt
8 egg whites
2 tsp ground nutmeg
4 tsp ground cinnamon
1 tsp ground cloves

In Indonesia, Lapis Legit is eaten usually at teatime. It also goes well with coffee, either mid-morning or after dinner. It should be sliced very thin and cut into pieces about 2 in (5 cm) long – it is very rich and the pieces must be small.

Beat the butter, vanilla and half the sugar until creamy. In another bowl, beat the egg yolks with the rest of the sugar until creamy and thick. Beat these mixtures together and add the milk. Sift the flour and salt into the bowl, and fold in carefully. Beat the egg whites until stiff and fold in.

Divide this mixture between two bowls. Stir the spices into one of them, so that you have one bowl coloured brown by the spices and the other cream-coloured.

Butter an 8–9 in (20–25 cm) square cake tin with a loose bottom. Heat the grill to its maximum temperature (if using a grill inside an oven, heat the oven to 150° C/275° F then turn it off before turning the grill on). Pour a layer of the cream batter, about ⅛ in (3 mm) thick, over the bottom. Grill this for a few minutes until the batter has set firm. Take out, and pour on the same thickness of the spiced, brown batter. Grill this as before. Continue this process, with alternate layers of brown and cream-coloured batter, until the batter is finished. (A good Lapis Legit will consist of 12–14 layers or more.) Transfer the cake to the oven and cook at 150° C/300° F/Gas Mark 2 for 10 minutes.

Remove the cake from the tin and cool on a wire rack.

Lapis Legit will keep moist and fresh in a cake tin or in the fridge for a week, well-wrapped in aluminium foil. It can also be frozen.

Putu Manis
Steamed coconut cup-cake

Makes 10–12 cups

5 eggs
4 tbs caster sugar
4 oz (120 g) rice flour
2 oz (50 g) plain flour
¼ pint (150 ml) thick coconut milk
a pinch of salt
2 tbs pandanus leaf juice (optional)
4 oz (120 g) grated coconut flesh

Traditionally Putu Manis is green. The green colour comes from the juice extracted from a fragrant leaf called daun pandan *(pandan or pandanus leaves).* Daun pandan *are now available in oriental shops in big cities. I like my Putu Manis white, so if you can't get the pandanus leaves, I suggest leaving them out rather than using food colouring.*

The normal cup used looks like an individual rum baba mould, so when you take your putu out it has a hole in the middle. But I use a Chinese tea cup without a handle, or a small ramekin.

To extract the juice from the pandanus leaves you need 4–5 leaves. Put these in a blender with 5 tablespoons water. Blend, then strain the juice.

One coconut will be sufficient for the quantities shown here. (See page 15 for notes on shelling coconuts and peeling off the brown skin). Peel one half and grate the flesh; use the other half, unpeeled, to make the coconut milk.

Beat the eggs and the sugar until thick and pale in colour. Add the flours, continue beating while you slowly add the coconut milk, salt and the pandanus leaf juice, if used. Beat the batter for about 3 more minutes.

Heat some water in a steamer; when boiling put in 10–12 cups to warm for 2 minutes.

Divide the grated coconut evenly between the cups, pressing it in with a spoon. Then pour in the batter, the same amount for each cup. Steam for 10 minutes. Turn out the cakes as soon as the cups are cool enough to handle. Putu Manis are normally eaten cold at tea-time.

Khanom Tuey
Coconut cups

Serves 6–8

6 fl oz (170 ml) coconut cream
4 oz (120 g) rice flour
3 tbs tapioca flour
*6 tbs grated palm sugar or dark soft
  brown sugar*
6 tbs cold water

FOR THE TOPPING
4 fl oz (120 ml) coconut cream
pinch of salt
2 tbs rice flour

This is a Thai sweet, similar to the Indonesian Kue Bugis which is wrapped in banana leaves for steaming. Khanom Tuey is made of ordinary rice flour topped with thick coconut cream, and is steamed in cups – again, the small Chinese teacups without handles are the best for this.

Mix the topping ingredients in a bowl and keep aside for later.

Sift the rice flour and tapioca flour together into a bowl. Pour the coconut cream, a little at a time, into the bowl containing the flours, kneading the flour with your hand. Knead for 2–3 minutes.

Put the sugar into a saucepan, heat until it melts, stir continuously for 1 minute, then add the water. Stir until the sugar is completely dissolved. Strain the syrup through a sieve into a bowl and leave to cool.

When cool, pour the syrup into the soft dough and mix well with a wooden spoon. Divide this batter among the cups, half-filling each cup. Steam in a double saucepan or steamer for 6 minutes. Add the topping to each cup and continue steaming for 2–3 minutes longer.

Serve warm or cold in the cup; eat with a small spoon.

Gula Melaka
Sago pudding

Serves 6–8

1 cup sago
1 cup water
1 cinnamon stick
3 oz (90 g) palm sugar
4 fl oz (120 ml)
1½ pints (900 ml) thick coconut milk
pinch of salt

FOR SERVING
8 fl oz (250 ml) gula melaka syrup,
*   made from about 6 oz (175 g) palm*
*   sugar*

This is very much like a sweet porridge, and in Indonesia we eat it as porridge for breakfast or as a snack at tea time. Gula melaka (palm sugar) is a coconut sugar, available now in the west in most oriental shops, packed in a small plastic container. Shave or chop this with a knife, or grate it on a hand grater, before putting it into the dish you are cooking.

Put the sago into a saucepan with a cup of water and the cinnamon; leave to soak while the other ingredients are being prepared. Chop the palm sugar, then dissolve over a very low heat with half a cup of water, and strain. Cook the sago by bringing the water to the boil and letting it simmer for about 3 minutes, stirring all the time. Add the coconut milk, salt and sugar syrup, and go on stirring for 10–15 minutes until the mixture becomes thick. Discard the cinnamon, and pour into a large bowl or several small bowls. Chill until the mixture is firm. It can be turned out of its mould or served in the small bowls where it has set; or you can spoon it out on to a dish, with the gula melaka syrup poured over it.

To make the syrup, boil the gula melaka for a few minutes in 8 fl oz (250 ml) of water, stirring continuously. Then strain through a fine sieve.

ACCOMPANIMENTS AND RELISHES

I suppose there ought to be a red triangle hoisted over this final section to warn the reader that some of these relishes are fairly hot – chilli-hot, or *pedas* as we say in Indonesian. But they don't have to be uncomfortably hot; in fact, they need not be hot at all if you don't want them to be. What many people overlook is that chilli peppers have a very characteristic strong, pungently smoky flavour, which is quite separate from their hotness. This flavour is the real purpose of many of the preparations that are described here. I have greatly reduced the quantity of chilli from what, in Indonesia and elsewhere, would be regarded as the barest minimum (except in the recipe for Sambal Ulek, which consists of little else but chilli, so I could hardly cut down there).

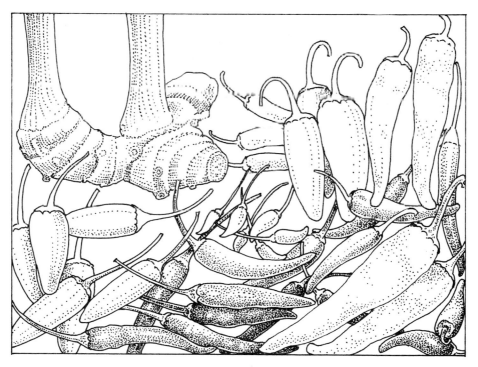

Chillies (different types and sizes), galingale

Sambal Ulek
Crushed red chillies with salt

Makes 2 lb (1 kg)

2 lb (1 kg) red chillies, stalks removed
1 pint (600 ml) cold water
1 tbs salt
1 tbs any vinegar
1 tsp sugar (optional)
2 tbs olive oil
4 tbs boiled water

This is the basis of all the sambals that Indonesians use, either as a hot relish or for spicing a cooked dish. You can buy this ready-made in jars from oriental shops as well as from large supermarkets. It is made in Holland, and labelled sambal oelek *(oe being the old spelling for* u*). For any recipe that specifies red chilli to be blended together with other spices, you can use sambal ulek instead. So when you can get fresh red chillies from Chinese or Indian shops, buy a lot and preserve them as sambal ulek. This will save you hunting around for chillies next time you need one. Sambal ulek can also be frozen and will keep for about 2 weeks or more in an airtight jar stored in the fridge.*

Put the chillies in a saucepan and cover with the water. Bring to the boil, then simmer for 15 minutes. Drain and put in a blender with the salt, vinegar and sugar (if used). Add the olive oil and boiled water, and blend until smooth. You may need to do this in batches.

Store in an airtight jar in the fridge, or pack in a plastic or aluminium container for the freezer.

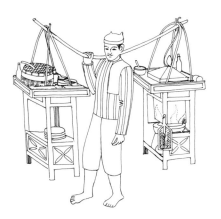

Sambal Bubuk Teri
Hot chilli relish with dried anchovies

1 lb (450 g) dried anchovies, heads
  removed
4 fl oz (120 ml) sunflower oil
½ oz (15 g) dried chillies, pounded, or
  chilli flakes
3 shallots, thinly sliced
3 cloves garlic, finely chopped
2 tbs sunflower oil

I almost decided not to include this recipe just because the name translates so long and awkwardly into English. But then I thought you might like to share my fondness for it, sprinkled on fried rice or fried noodles. It is also good on an omelette, an egg sandwich or a pizza. Ikan teri (or, as the Malaysians call them, ikan bilis) are sold in packets of 8 oz (225 g) or 1 lb (450 g), with heads on. You need to remove the heads to make your sambal taste good.

Heat the 4 fl oz (120 ml) oil in a wok or frying pan, and fry the dried anchovies in 2 or 3 batches, stirring continuously, for 4 minutes each time. Remove with a slotted spoon into a colander lined with kitchen paper. Leave to cool, then pound in a mortar with a pestle until the anchovies are coarsely ground-up.

Discard the oil and wipe the wok or frying pan clean with kitchen paper. Heat the 2 tbs clean oil, fry the pounded dried chilli or flakes together with the sliced shallots and chopped garlic, stirring continuously, for 2–3 minutes. Then add the pounded anchovies, and stir for another minute. Remove to a plate lined with kitchen paper and leave to cool. Store in an airtight container for up to 2 weeks.

Goreng Bawang
Fried shallots

Makes 2 lb (1 kg)

2 lb (1 kg) shallots, thinly sliced
½ pint (300 ml) sunflower oil

Both the Indonesians and the Thais use crispy fried shallots as a garnish on rice, dry-fried meat and many other dishes. You can use onions instead of shallots if you wish; as they contain more water than shallots, it is a good idea to sprinkle them with flour before frying. However, I personally wouldn't bother to make my own fried onions, when you can buy very good ones from Denmark so cheaply in the shops here. Fried shallots are something different.

It is a lot easier if you have a wok to fry these, but a frying pan will do.

Heat the oil until a sliver of shallot dropped into it sizzles immediately. Fry the shallots in 3 or 4 batches, stirring continuously, for 3–4 minutes until they are crisp and slightly brown. Remove with a slotted spoon to drain in a colander lined with absorbent paper. Let them cool before storing in an airtight container. They will keep fresh and crisp in the container for about 1 week.

Goreng Teri Dan Kacang
Crisp fried anchovies with peanuts

1 lb (450 g) dried anchovies, heads
  removed
1 lb (450 g) peanuts
4 fl oz (120 ml) sunflower oil or peanut oil
½ tsp chilli powder (optional)

See Sambal Bubuk Teri on page 119 for an explanation of dried anchovies. You'll be more likely to find this relish in Malaysian restaurants than in Indonesian ones. At home, we serve fried peanuts and anchovies separately, but in London I go along with the Malaysians because dried anchovies are quite expensive and mixing them with the relatively cheap peanuts makes sense. They are also very good to serve with drinks.

In a wok or frying pan heat the oil and fry the peanuts in 3 batches, stirring continuously, for 4 minutes each time. Remove with a slotted spoon to drain in a colander or on a plate lined with kitchen paper. Use the same oil to fry the dried anchovies in 3 batches, for 3–4 minutes each time. Drain in the same way. Allow to go cold, then mix well together and put in an airtight container. Add the chilli powder (if using) and shake well to mix. Keeps for up to 2 weeks.

121

Sambal Kacang/Bumbu Sate
Peanut sauce/Saté sauce

4 fl oz (120 ml) vegetable oil
8 oz (225 g) raw peanuts
2 cloves garlic, chopped
4 shallots, chopped
1/2 in (1 cm) piece of shrimp paste
salt to taste
1/2 tsp chilli powder
1/2 tsp brown sugar
1 tbs dark soya sauce
16 fl oz (500 ml) water
1 tbs tamarind water or juice of 1/2
  lemon

This well-known peanut sauce for saté is not difficult to make and it is really not necessary to use crunchy peanut butter. It won't be easier that way, it will merely cost more as peanut butter is more expensive than raw peanuts. But if you like chilli-hot peanut sauce you can buy, in most Chinese or oriental shops, a ready-prepared powdered 'satay sauce' mix.

In a wok or frying pan, heat the oil, and fry the peanuts, stirring all the time, for 4 minutes. Remove with a slotted spoon to drain in a colander. Leave to cool. When cool, pound or grind the peanuts into a fine powder, using a blender, coffee grinder or pestle and mortar. Discard the oil except for 1 tbs.

Crush the garlic, shallots and shrimp paste in a mortar with a little salt. Fry in the remaining oil for 1 minute. Add the chilli powder, sugar, soya sauce, then add the water. Bring this mixture to the boil, and stir in the ground peanuts. Simmer, stirring occasionally, until the sauce becomes thick; this should take about 8–10 minutes. Add the tamarind water or lemon juice and more salt if necessary.

When cool, keep in a jar in the fridge. Reheat as required to use for saté or as a dip for crudités or other savoury snacks. Will keep for up to 1 week in the fridge.

Sambal Tomat
Tomato sauce

2 tbs sunflower oil
4 shallots, sliced
1 in (2½ cm) root ginger, finely
   chopped
½ in (1 cm) piece of shrimp paste
   (optional)
3 (or fewer) red chillies, seeded and
   chopped, or 1 tsp sambal ulek (page
   118)
8 fl oz (250 ml) water
1 lb (450 g) red tomatoes or canned
   tomatoes
1 tsp salt
1 tsp sugar

Like all other sambals, Indonesian tomato sauce is usually chilli-hot, but in this book, as I am suggesting it for general use, I make it quite mild. By all means add more chillies if you want it hot.

In a wok or small saucepan heat the oil and fry the shallots, ginger and shrimp paste, mashing the shrimp paste with a wooden spoon and stirring continuously, for 1–2 minutes. Add the chillies or sambal ulek, stir again for 1 minute, then add the water, tomatoes, salt and sugar.

Bring to the boil, then simmer for 10 minutes or until the tomatoes are well cooked. Mash the tomatoes roughly with the wooden spoon. The sambal is now just as we would use it as sambal in Indonesia. However, if you want a smooth sauce, pass it through a sieve into another saucepan.

Adjust the seasoning and heat again for 1 minute if you want to serve the sauce hot, for instance to pour over the Tod Man Muh (page 66). This sauce can be served, hot or cold, as a dip.

Nam Chim
Sweet and sour chilli sauce

1 lb (450 g) red chillies, seeded and
  chopped
2 cloves garlic, chopped
2 tbs water
2 tbs peanut oil or olive oil
4 tbs grated palm sugar or granulated
  sugar
6 tbs white malt vinegar
2 tsp salt
8 fl oz (250 ml) water

This Thai sauce is widely available in bottles in most oriental shops, but it is quite easy to make. It is used as a dip for snacks or grilled fish, stuffed chicken wings, etc.

Put the chillies, garlic, 2 tbs water and oil in a blender and blend until smooth. Put the remaining ingredients in a saucepan and add the chilli paste. Bring to the boil and simmer for 30–40 minutes, or until reduced by half. Leave to cool before storing in a jar or bottle. Will keep fresh in the fridge for at least 2 weeks.

Sambal Kecap
Soya sauce with chilli

2–4 small chillies, seeded and finely
  chopped
2 shallots, finely sliced
1 clove garlic, finely chopped (optional)
juice of 1 small lime or lemon
1 tsp olive oil (optional)
1 tbs light soya sauce
1 tbs dark soya sauce

This sauce is particularly good for saté, especially for those who do not like peanut sauce. It is very easy and quick to prepare – lovely to dip crispy and crunchy miniature spring rolls into (page 28), to spoon lightly over fried noodles, or to use as a dip for crunchy raw vegetables, such as carrots and celery.

Mix all the ingredients in a bowl and put on the table for everybody to share; or serve in small individual bowls as a dip for miniature spring rolls or saté.

Krupuk Udang Dan Emping
Prawn crackers and emping crackers

Both these crackers are used to accompany food or as snacks to serve with drinks. They can be bought uncooked in many Oriental and Chinese shops. The best krupuk are 'Krupuk Sidoarjo', which are made in Indonesia, imported by the Dutch and then re-exported to other countries in western Europe. The Thais also make excellent prawn crackers. You can safely assume that emping are vegetarian crisps, since they are made of a nut called melinjo. *They vary in size, but the ones available in the west are quite small, and they don't get much bigger when fried. Choose a packet that still contains plenty of whole emping rather than one which has too many broken tiny pieces. They are quite brittle and get crushed easily.*

To fry krupuk or emping you need a wok or a deep frying pan (a deep fryer is not suitable). The ideal temperature is 180° C/350° F. Fry the krupuk one at a time, rocking each one gently with a spatula as soon as it is in the hot oil. You need another tool to hold the rapidly-expanding krupuk so that it comes out more or less flat. Leave to cool a little to make it crisp and delicious.

Emping can be fried a handful at a time. Stir them continuously, and remove them from the oil with a large slotted spoon as soon as they have turned colour a little – this will take about 20 seconds.

Both krupuk and emping will keep crisp in airtight containers for at least 2 weeks.

BIBLIOGRAPHY

Jennifer Brennan, *Thai Cooking*, Jill Norman & Hobhouse, London, 1981

Alan Davidson, *South-East Asian Seafood*, Federal Publications, Singapore, 1977, and Macmillan, London, 1978

Clifford Geertz, *Negara: The Theatre State in Nineteenth-Century Bali*, Princeton University Press, Princeton NJ, 1980

Clifford Geertz, *The Religion of Java*, The Free Press, 1960; reprinted by University of Chicago Press, Chicago

Elisabeth Lambert Ortiz, *Caribbean Cookery*, André Deutsch, London, 1975, and Penguin Books, 1977

Sri Owen, *Indonesian Food and Cookery*, (2nd edn.) Prospect Books, London, 1986

Mustika Rasa: Buku Masakan Indonesia, Departemen Pertanian, Jakarta, 1967

William Shurtleff and Akiko Aoyagi, *The Book of Tempeh*, Harper and Row, New York, 1979

Phia Sing, *Traditional Recipes of Laos*, Prospect Books, London, 1981

M. L. Taw Kritakara and M. R. Pimsai Amranand, *Modern Thai Cooking*, Editions Duang Kamol, Bangkok, 1977

The two books by Clifford Geertz are obviously not cookery books; they contain some interesting background information about food cultivation, cooking and eating in Bali and Java.

Acknowledgement

The *Homok Talay* illustrated in this book was cooked by chefs at the Blue Elephant, London SW6, and the pot and plate were also supplied by the Blue Elephant.

The white plates in the *Kratong Thong* and *Fried Miniature Spring Rolls* illustration were supplied by Kitchens Etcetera, High Street, Wimbledon Village.

INDEX

Recipe titles have been set in *italics*.
Only major references are given for common ingredients.
NB Indonesian *c* is pronounced as *ch* in *church*.